# HEAD-TO-TOE HEALING:

## *Your Body's Repair Manual*

# HEAD-TO-TOE HEALING:
## *Your Body's Repair Manual*

Chunyi Lin

SFQ
SPRING FOREST QIGONG

The information in this book and all Spring Forest Qigong teaching and learning materials is intended for education about healthful practices. It is not intended as a replacement for any medical treatment or therapy prescribed by a physician or other licensed health care provider, but is intended to help you broaden your understanding of health and wellness and make informed choices about health options. Any application of the information in this book and in other Spring Forest Qigong materials is at your discretion and is your sole responsibility.

## SFQ
SPRING FOREST QIGONG

Published by Spring Forest Qigong
www.springforestqigong.com

ISBN 9780-9801089-6-5

First Edition
Printed in the United States of America

Cover Design by RAD Designs LLC.
Book Design and Layout by Andrea Wallace
    and Rick Wallace
Illustrations by Rick Wallace, Andrea
    Wallace, and Audrey Wallace
Edited by Susan Bundlie, Patrick Dougherty
    and Laura Phillips

# Contents

## PREFACE

A few weeks ago I was being interviewed on a radio talk show, and the host absolutely amazed me. Many years earlier he had been diagnosed with terminal cancer. Doctors gave him no hope but, he refused to accept that.

He said he just knew instinctively that if his body had created this disease, his body could get rid of it. So that's what he set out to do. He focused the power of his mind on purging the cancer from his body. He told me he believed with all his heart that not only was it possible, it was inevitable. And so it was.

Within months, through the power of his mind and the belief in his heart, the cancer was gone from his body. His doctors had no explanation. They were absolutely amazed. And he remains cancer free to this day.

At the time he didn't know anything about energy medicine or qigong. He intuitively knew that his body was designed to heal itself. It just made perfect sense to him.

If you stop and think about it, you'll quickly realize that if our bodies weren't designed to heal themselves, then the human race wouldn't have lasted very long.

Every technique you will find in this book is designed to stimulate your body's natural healing abilities. These techniques are based on principles that date back thousands of years and have been refined over the millennia.

This is not the first healing story of its kind that I've heard. I've heard many, and they are all very powerful. I share this story with you in hopes of inspiring you, and I hope I have. The power of your mind and the power of your heart are truly extraordinary.

Through your heart you are connected to what Gandhi called "the most powerful force the world possesses," the power of unconditional love. I encourage you to focus on this power in your heart whenever you are using these techniques.

It is not necessary for you to believe in any of this in order to benefit from these techniques. The techniques themselves are designed to stimulate your body's healing energy.

All that you really need is an open mind and a willingness to do something new. Give it a try and you may be amazed.

With love and blessings,

Chunyi Lin
International Qigong Master
Founder and Chairman of Spring Forest Qigong

# INTRODUCTION

Did you know that your body is designed to be healthy? Did you know that when you have an illness or any physical problem, your body has an innate wisdom it uses to try to heal itself? And did you know that you have the ability to greatly enhance your body's capacity to heal and to stay healthy?

Modern medicine offers us an incredible array of health care to help us through the simplest to the most complex health challenges. It is especially beneficial in times of pressing critical medical need. Most of us have access to doctors, urgent care centers, and even specialists if the need should arise.

But you may be finding that your resources, or those of your health care plan, are limited. Maybe what you are looking for regarding your health care concerns is just not offered through standard health care. You may find yourself, along with millions of others, searching for self-empowering complementary practices that are credible and user friendly to aid in healing and maintaining your health. This book can be your guide.

Since the beginning of time people have used different healing and health care techniques and practices. From shamans to medicine men and women, from those proficient in adjusting bones to those who knew how to attend to wounds and suggest herbs to take for different ailments, help has been given, prescriptions have been offered, and techniques have been taught to promote healing. All have sought to use the body's innate wisdom to help itself heal.

Many of these practices were primitive and marginally effective by today's standards, yet a few have withstood the ages and continue to offer simple and effective help in healing the body. Perhaps none is as well known as those techniques that have come out of Traditional Chinese Medicine (TCM)— techniques that have been practiced and refined for thousands of years and are still prescribed on a regular basis.

Most of these come from a branch of TCM called "qigong." Qigong, which translates into "the function of energy" or "energy work," teaches you techniques to help aid the flow of energy in your body to promote healing and health. This book is a compilation of some of the simplest and most effective qigong techniques known.

**Please note:** *If you are under a doctor's care or in any type of ongoing treatment, please continue to follow that plan. The techniques in this book are meant to be complementary.*

## SPRING FOREST QIGONG—WHO WE ARE

Spring Forest Qigong (SFQ) is a simple, effective, and efficient form of qigong developed to help you find health, balance, and energy to meet today's challenges. Whether you come to SFQ because you want to know just enough to help yourself with a specific issue or you intend to become a serious student, you quickly learn how simple it is to help yourself and others heal and maintain optimal health.

More than 120,000 students have taken our classes and have been taught the Spring Forest Qigong method as well as many other simple health-enhancing techniques. The number of people who have benefited from these techniques has grown exponentially. The students and the thousands of people who have come through our healing center have found it easy to teach the techniques to their friends and family members—something you will probably find yourself doing too. This book is written partly in response to our students' requests to compile simple and clear instructions to have as a handy guide when one of those everyday healing needs arises.

What distinguishes SFQ from other qigong schools—and something that its founder, Master Chunyi Lin, is adamant about—is its simplicity. SFQ teaches that you were born a healer. You have the capacity to significantly impact your own health by practicing simple qigong exercises and techniques to heal current problems and to prevent future ones. You also have the ability to do simple qigong techniques to help others heal. There is nothing fancy or complicated to learn; you can do so much by doing so little. You just need the information, and that is what this book is about.

We draw on ancient universal wisdom, Traditional Chinese Medicine (TCM), and qigong practices to teach you simple techniques you can do to help yourself and others heal and maintain optimal health. SFQ is designed for you to use what you like and what feels best for you and to forget what doesn't help. Just use the techniques that make sense to you, or adapt them as you see fit or as your body tells you to.

## HOW TO USE THIS BOOK

The "Traditional Chinese Medicine" section below explains some of the basics about TCM. If you know about the energetic body, meridians, and acupuncture points, you may find this section valuable as a quick review, or you can just skip it. If you don't know much about the energetic body or TCM, this will be a very useful guide to help you learn the basics.

Following the TCM information is a section entitled "Important terms and concepts" which explains several things that will be important for you to know. It also has some of the finer points about TCM and how we interpret them.

The actual healing techniques are written in a specific order. We start by giving you a deep breathing technique and then move on to healing techniques performed on various parts of your body from your head down to your toes. Because of the connections between body meridians /channels and body organs, the spot where a technique is performed does not necessarily correspond physically to the ailment you are trying to believe. For example, there is a specific technique you can use to help your digestive system, but it's performed nowhere near that area—it's done on your lips. You will want to use these techniques to work specifically on areas of concern preventatively and/or when you have a specific condition or illness.

## Index

The alphabetical index in the back of the book is designed to help you find the right technique. If you are fatigued, your baby is crying, or you have stomach pains, the index will help you quickly find the most beneficial techniques for your concern.

If you have a headache, for example, you will find page numbers listed after "Headaches" that will lead you to specific techniques you can use to relieve your pain. Note that you will find them arranged in numerical order rather than order of effectiveness, since each person's needs differ.

Trust yourself and trust your body. People respond more positively to some of these techniques than they do to others, and it is very important that you learn to listen to yourself regarding what your body likes and needs at any particular time. Some techniques might feel very beneficial to you, others could feel like they may or may not be helping, and still others might seem to provide no benefit at all. Practice those techniques that your body tells you it likes.

## Chant sounds (Appendix A)

With some of the healing techniques there is a suggested sound to chant. Throughout history, chanting, singing, or using sound in some manner has been a common technique for enhancing health and healing. In SFQ we see sound as one of the four elements that aid healing; the other three are breathing, postures, and the mind.

Some people like to use these sounds, while others do not. If you choose to use them, first chant the sound six times quietly enough that only you can hear it, then do it silently as many times as you'd like. Chanting is not essential, however. At Spring Forest Qigong we believe that when you are doing qigong, or using these techniques, there is no right or wrong way to do them. There is only good, better, or best.

The chanting will enhance the effectiveness of the technique; however, doing the technique as we describe, without the chanting, will still be very beneficial.

You will find more information about the chant sounds, and how to pronounce them, in Appendix A.

If you do not feel comfortable doing the chants after reading about them, and you would like to know more, look for them on our website: www.springforestqigong.com.

## Lifestyles (Appendix B)

In Appendix B three common lifestyles are listed that can, and commonly do, cause energy blockages:

- **Sitting at a keyboard all day**
- **Being on your feet a lot**
- **Doing physically strenuous labor**

We suggest some techniques to help ease the daily stress of each of these lifestyles and to help prevent or treat current conditions.

## TRADITIONAL CHINESE MEDICINE (TCM)

If you know about the energetic body, meridians, and acupuncture points, you may find this section valuable as a quick review. If you don't know much about the energetic body or TCM, this will be a very useful guide to help you learn the basics—just as much as you need to know about TCM to make sense of this book. Everything we mention below will be revisited in the healing techniques section of the book.

The Chinese believe that everything in the universe is comprised of a balance of two energies: yin and yang. Sometimes seen as opposites, these energies are always complementary and always present. After a few thousand years of research and practice, TCM has found that there is an energy ("qi" or "chi," pronounced "chee") flowing through the channels ("meridians") in your body. Maintaining a healthy flow of qi through your meridians helps keep the yin and yang energy in balance and promotes good health.

There are 12 primary meridians in your body and 8 "extraordinary" or "reservoir" channels, as well as other energy pathways. Two of the extraordinary channels are believed to be the most important. Both start at the "lower dantian," an important energy center that is deep in behind your navel. One basically goes up the center of the front of your body and stops at the bottom of your mouth, and the other runs down to the bottom of your body, up your spine, over your head, and stops at the roof of your mouth. From the 12 primary meridians, energy travels through your limbs and torso to your organs.

Blockage in any of the meridians will cause a disruption of energy flow in your body that will result in physical or mental health difficulties. Imagine a river becoming blocked. The blockage can cause problems, some very serious, until it is cleared and the natural flow of water is restored. That is what much of TCM is about—opening up blockages and restoring the natural flow of energy through the meridians. It is also what this book is about.

Acupuncture is one treatment modality that comes out of TCM and is probably the best-known method of opening blockages and restoring flow and balance to the body. A trained professional does this treatment to you as a patient. There are also two methods you can do to yourself: acupressure, which is like acupuncture but using fingers instead of needles, and qigong. In fact, Chunyi Lin has created a specific acupressure technique called Qi~ssage that combines massage and acupressure techniques with qigong.

A central aspect of qigong that is a significant element in some of these techniques is that what your mind thinks about you—your body, your mental health, your self worth—affects your physical and mental health.

Because everything is energy, the images and stories your mind creates are energy. When you have thoughts about yourself, your thoughts send out an energy message to your body—either positive, negative, or neutral—and your body is impacted. In qigong, and in this book, the power of your mind is used to help you send out healing messages and to aid your healing process.

To summarize, TCM and its different methods of treatment are all meant to enhance or restore the flow of energy through your body. The techniques in this book are all simple techniques to help open specific blockages or to stimulate certain organs and restore the flow of energy through your meridians. You can do this to help treat specific conditions or to help prevent problems and maintain health.

An interesting and exciting note: Western science is beginning to embrace the understanding that people are energy beings, especially when it comes to the power of the mind and how our thinking affects all aspects of our lives. Dr. Bruce Lipton, author of The Biology of Belief, teaches that your genes do not control your life, as has long been thought to be true, but that they are just a blueprint for your life. It is the influence of your environment, as well as the energetic impact of your perceptions and beliefs, which affect you physically, mentally, and emotionally. Also, Candice Pert, Ph.D., renowned neuroscientist and pharmacologist and author of Molecules of Emotion, has found that your cells are in a constant energetic vibration and are affected by your thoughts and your environment. On the SFQ website's medical research page, you will find much more information, including a recent study from the Mayo Clinic about qigong and chronic pain: www.springforestqigong.com/research.

## IMPORTANT TERMS AND CONCEPTS

If you are reading one of the healing techniques and are confused about what we mean, you will probably find clarity in the section below.

### Universal energy

The universe and everything in it is comprised of two kinds of energy: yin and yang. It is believed that the universe holds a harmony or perfect balance of these two energies, and this is often called "the harmony of the universe." We humans are often out of balance with yin and yang energies, which is what leads to physical, emotional, and spiritual problems. To seek good health, pursue healing, and help us find a healthy flow in our lives, we need to return to a balance of yin and yang by aligning or reconnecting with the harmony of the universe.

### The power of your mind in sending positive messages

In TCM, as in most health practices of the East and a growing number in the West, it is believed that your mind plays an integral role in your health. Your thoughts, which are also energy, are constantly sending your body messages that are positive, negative, or neutral. Research tells us that people with a positive attitude toward life live longer and live healthier. We know it is difficult to change your thought patterns quickly, but even sending a positive message for five seconds can have a beneficial impact. We suggest that whenever you are working with one of the techniques you send a positive message to the part of your body that needs healing, telling it that it is restored to perfect health or that it remains in perfect health.

### Good, better, or best

It is very normal for people in the West to think that if they don't do something just right, then they are doing it wrong. That is not the case with qigong or with these techniques. We suggest you look at doing these techniques (and for that matter, everything in your life) as either good, better, or best. You cannot do these techniques wrong—especially when in your mind you are telling yourself you are doing them just wonderfully and are visualizing the great benefits you are getting.

## The lower dantian

In TCM, the lower dantian is the main energy center in the body. It is located deep in behind the navel and is where vital "qi," or energy, is cultivated and stored; from here it can be directed and channeled throughout the body.

## Listening to your body

Your body has its own wisdom that might be different from the wisdom we offer. It actually may even be directly opposed to what we say and what is effective for other people. Taking responsibility for your own health makes you the primary care person in charge. From a qigong perspective it is believed that you are the best doctor you can have, because you know and can listen to your body better than anyone else.

Certainly if you are under a doctor's care or in any type of ongoing treatment, please continue to follow that plan. Spring Forest Qigong is a complementary practice, and these techniques are meant to be the same. But do listen to your body so you can increase your trust in knowing what it needs.

## Putting a smile on your face

Think of a true smile—not an artificial or plastic smile, but one that comes from your heart or from happiness; that is how we want you to smile. This simple gesture is very powerful. First, it begins to open your heart and makes a connection between your mind energy and your heart energy. Then it helps lead to a release of endorphins, giving a sense of well-being that is powerful for healing. It is good to do this with every technique we offer.

## Massaging technique

Many of the techniques in the book suggest you massage a certain point or area. Unless otherwise noted, you do this with a pressure that is firm, yet gentle. You want to stimulate the area, but not so much that it hurts.

We often say to put your finger on a certain point and massage in a circular manner. Your finger gently moves in a circular way without leaving the spot. Your skin might move a little, or a muscle or tendon might move, but your finger stays on the spot you first touched.

## How long and how often to practice a specific technique

We get quite specific about how long and how often to practice each of the techniques. For most of them, however, we suggest you do it as long as seems right to you. The first couple of times you do a specific technique, if possible, don't think about how long we tell you to do it or how much time you have in your schedule to practice it. Try to really listen to your body, and it will let you know when you have done it long enough. Then use this as your standard.

The same is true about how often you do it. Try to listen to when your body would like you to do the technique. If your body isn't giving you a clear message, and you don't have an intuitive sense, then follow our recommendation. Think "good, better, and best."

## The best time to practice these techniques

We do suggest specific times to practice these techniques, and we do this for a simple reason: the channels or meridians in your body respond differently at different times of the day. That is why we suggest you do some techniques in the morning or evening, as they will be a little more effective at those times. But all of these techniques will be good for you whenever you practice them.

# Healing Techniques

All Ages

# 01 BREATHING, DEEP

## HELPS WITH

- Decreasing stress
- Improving digestion
- Enhancing your immune system
- Improving just about everything else that ails you

## HOW

Relax your shoulders. Relax your body. Gently inhale and exhale through your nose. Your breath should be deep, slow, and quiet. If your breathing is shallow, gently increase the amount of your inhale a bit, and then gently increase the amount of your exhale. Go slowly and don't work hard as you improve your breathing because that would create stress.

Here is a simple exercise that can help you learn to breathe better: As you inhale, visualize your breath as a ball of white energy coming in through your nose and going down past your lungs to an area deep in behind your navel (this is the area the Chinese call the "lower dantian"). See the white ball brighten every time you inhale. Then relax as you exhale.

### Best Time

Every moment of your life

### Why

*The deeper you breathe, the more oxygen you get into your lungs. More oxygen getting into your lungs means more oxygen getting into your blood; because of this, most systems in your body are going to work much more efficiently than they would if you breathed shallowly.*

*Inhaling slowly and deeply sends more energy to heal your sympathetic nervous system, which is concerned with preparing your body to react to situations of stress or emergency by accelerating your heart rate, constricting your blood vessels, and raising your blood pressure.*

*Exhaling slowly and completely gives a signal to your parasympathetic nervous system to help it detoxify more deeply. This system serves to slow the rate and force of your heartbeat, decreases your blood pressure, and enhances your digestion.*

# 02 HEAD, TOP OF

## HELPS WITH

- Anxiety
- Strokes
- Parkinson's Disease
- Headaches

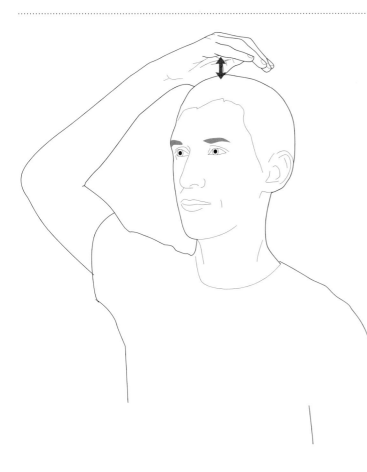

## HOW

Hold your hand like a cup, as if it were holding water. Either hand will do. Gently pat (cup) the top of your head (for a headache you may cup very softly).

While you are cupping, see golden light shooting into the top of your head and reaching the middle of your head. Visualize putting a healing message in that light, such as "The anxiety is gone; peace is present," or "My headache is gone, totally gone." Remember to take slow, deep, peaceful breaths. While you are cupping, chant the sound "kerrr."

### *How Long*
Three minutes

### *How Often*
Three times a day or as needed

### *Best Time*
Morning or anytime

### *Why*
*The top of your head has an energy point called "Baihui." All your body's yang energy channels converge here. Cupping this point stimulates energy in your brain and your head and activates energy in your body. It also helps release pressure and brings excess energy down into your body.*

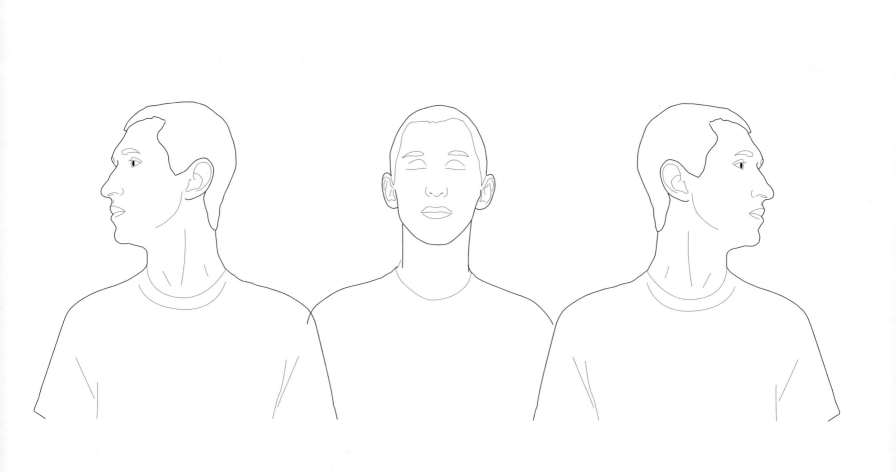

# 03 HEAD AND NECK

## HELPS WITH

- Headaches
- Heart disease
- Lung congestion
- Eye diseases
- Stress release in head, neck, and shoulders

**HOW**

Sit or stand straight, facing forward, with your eyes closed. Slowly turn your head to the left. When your head is turned as far as it comfortably can turn, quickly open your eyes and look into the distance for about one second. (It is good to imagine looking across a great distance. If you are in a room, imagine seeing a mountain range or a forest or something similar in the distance.)

Now close your eyes again and slowly turn your head to the right. When your head has moved to the right as far as it comfortably can, quickly open your eyes and look far into the distance for one second. Chant the sound "kerrr."

Repeat nine times.

*How Long*
Enough time to complete nine rotations

*How Often*
Three times a day or as needed

*Best Time*
In the morning, but anytime is good

---

*Why*
This exercise helps open a better connection between your eyes, your brain, and the rest of your body. It also stimulates energy channels to your lungs and heart, activates the energy in your eyes, strengthens the muscles in your neck, and releases stress in your head, neck, and shoulders.

# 04 HEAD, BASE OF

## HELPS WITH

- Hearing loss
- Ringing in ears
- Colds
- Opening sinuses

- Poor memory
- Headache
- Dizziness/vertigo
- Motion sickness

## HOW

Holding one hand as a cup, slightly bend your head forward, and gently pat (cup) the base of your head where your spine goes into your skull. Chant the sound "kerrr."

### How Long
Two to three minutes

### How Often
Two to three times a day

### Best Time
Anytime

### Why
There are many energy points in this area affecting your eyes, speech, sinuses, hearing, mouth, and your entire brain. Cupping this way helps bring clarity to your mind, prevents colds, and keeps your sinuses open.

# 05 FOREHEAD

## HELPS WITH

- Insomnia
- Headache
- Eye fatigue
- Mental clarity

## HOW

Use your middle finger to massage, in a circular fashion, the point in the center of your forehead directly between your eyebrows and just above the bridge of your nose. Chant the sound "kerrr."

### How Long

Two minutes or more, especially if you can't sleep

### How Often

As needed

### Best Time

Anytime

> ### Why
> This point connects to your eyes and to specific parts of your brain. Massaging here can bring peace if your brain has been overactive.

# 06 EYEBROWS

## HELPS WITH

- Nearsightedness and farsightedness
- Glaucoma
- Migraine headaches
- Allergies

**HOW**

Put a thumb on each temple, curve your fingers, and—as firmly as is comfortable for you—draw the sides of the middle knuckles of your index fingers along your eyebrows from the inside edge to the outside edge.

Next draw the sides of the middle knuckles of your index fingers along the bone under your eyes. Alternate between massaging your eyebrows and massaging the bone under your eyes in this manner.

Put a smile on your face. See golden light in the areas you massage and visualize a healing message going into that light, such as "I see perfectly" or "My head feels fine." Chant the sound "sheee."

Repeat nine times.

### How Long
Five minutes is best, less time is fine

### How Often
Two times a day

### Best Time
In the morning and early evening

### Why
*There are many energy points in these areas that connect directly to your eyes as well as to your lungs, liver, and many other organs.*

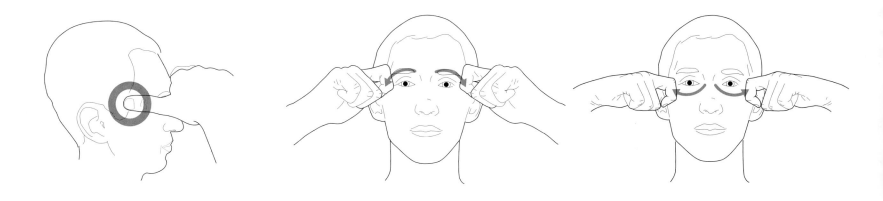

# 07 TEMPLES

## HELPS WITH
- Clarity of thinking
- Headaches
- Stress
- Stimulation of immune system
- Insomnia

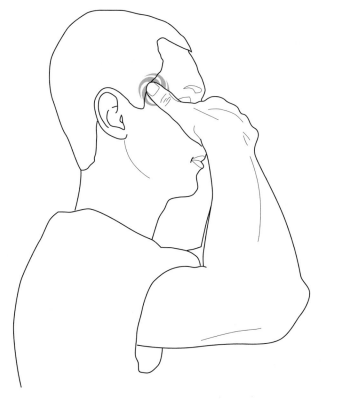

## HOW
Place your thumbs on your temples and gently but firmly massage in a circular way in one direction 36 times; then massage the other direction 36 times. One circle should take about one second. Chant the sound "kerrr."

### How Long
One to two minutes—one set of 36 in each direction is good; more sets are better

### How Often
As needed

### Best Time
Anytime

> ### Why
> In your temples there are powerful energy points and nerve systems connecting directly to certain parts of your brain. Massaging here helps balance your brain's energy, enhancing its circulation and reducing its stress.

# 08 EYES, CIRCLING OF

## HELPS WITH

- Motion sickness
- Glaucoma
- Allergy reactions in your eyes
- Crossed eyes
- "Lazy eye"

## HOW

Sit up straight, look forward, and relax. Move your eyes in a circle three times one way, then three times the other way. Chant the sound "sheee."

### How Long
One minute

### How Often
As needed

### Best Time
Anytime

> ### Why
> Your eyes have many energetic and nerve connections to your brain, to other parts of your head, and to your heart and liver. This exercise promotes healthy eyes.

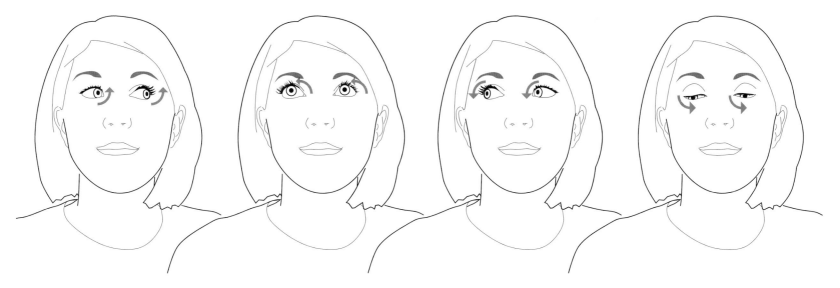

# 09 EYES, PALMING OF

## HELPS WITH
- Nearsightedness and farsightedness
- Glaucoma
- Macular degeneration

## HOW
Rub your palms together until they are very warm and then place them over each eye, as shown in the illustration. Visualize and feel the heat penetrating deeply into your eyes while you send a healing message, such as "My nearsightedness is gone" or "My vision is perfect." Hold your palms like this for as long as you like—one to two minutes is usually good.

### How Long
One to two minutes, repeating as many times as you'd like

### How Often
One time a day or more

### Best Time
Anytime

### Why
The heat and energy from your palms stimulates, relaxes, and opens up channels in your eyes. Your eyes do so much work but get so little attention. They love this exercise for healing and maintaining their health.

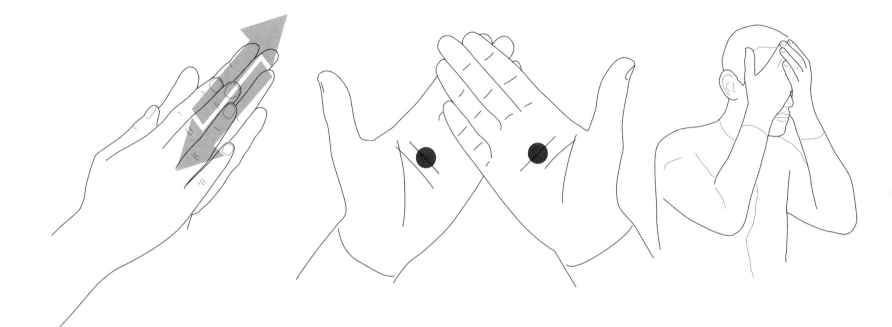

# 10 EYES, UNDER

## HELPS WITH
- Diabetes
- Poor eyesight
- Candida
- Blood sugar problems

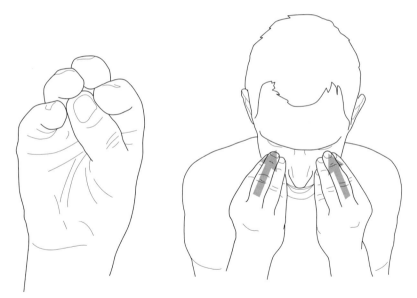

## HOW
Bunch your five fingers together so the tips form a circle. With both hands, firmly tap the areas under your eyes right below the bone of your eye socket. If this is not convenient because of your fingernails, use just your middle finger to tap or gently massage the area. The vibration of this movement helps to open the channels. Chant the sound "whooo."

### How Long
Three minutes each time

### How Often
As often as you'd like

### Best Time
Anytime is good; morning is best

> ### Why
> These areas have energy points connecting directly to the stomach channels. Tapping here will improve your digestive system and help alleviate problems associated with your stomach channels, such as diabetes and blood sugar issues.

# 11 NOSE, SIDES OF

## HELPS WITH

- Allergies
- Stuffy or runny nose
- Colds
- Vision problems

## HOW

Place the index and middle fingers of each hand near the bottom of each side of your nose, and gently massage by pushing your fingers up along the sides to the top of your nose and then drawing them down to the corners of your mouth. Chant the sound "seee."

### How Long
One minute or more

### How Often
As needed

### Best Time
Morning or evening is best; anytime is good

### Why
*Along your nose there are many energy points connecting to your sinuses and also to your head, lungs, liver, and other organs. Massaging here helps to stimulate and open these points.*

# 12 NOSE, TIP OF

## HELPS WITH

- High blood pressure
- Recovery from heart attack
- Helps cleanse excessive iron from the walls of your veins and arteries

## HOW

Rub your hands together until they are warm, place the middle of your left palm on the tip of your nose, and massage in one direction for 36 circles (move your nose gently, but firmly—it should not hurt). Then rub your hands together again until they are warm, place your right palm on your nose, and massage the other direction 36 times. Chant the sound "kerrr."

### How Long

One set of 36 in each direction is good; more sets are better

### How Often

As needed

### Best Time

At noon is best; anytime is good

### Why

*The tip of your nose has energy points connecting to your heart. Massaging here will promote the overall wellness of your heart by strengthening its muscles and enhancing its blood circulation.*

# 13 NOSE, BELOW

## HELPS WITH

- Fainting
- Seizures
- Restoring consciousness
- Mental clarity

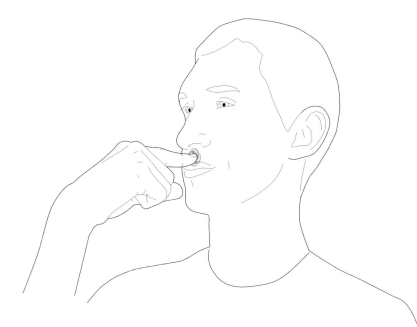

## HOW

Using the tip of your index or your middle finger, massage the area right below your nose by pressing gently, but firmly, and moving your finger slightly in any direction. You can do this to yourself if you feel like you are about to faint or experience a seizure, or you can do this to another person who is unconscious (after, of course, you have called for medical assistance). Chant the sound "kerrr."

### How Long

One minute.

In an emergency, if a person is unconscious, use your thumb to press this point firmly and deeply for about two to five minutes.

### How Often

As needed

### Best Time

Anytime

### Why

*Massaging here stimulates an important energy point that connects to a nerve in your brain. This can "wake up" and stimulate the energy throughout your brain to aid healing and bring balance.*

# 14 LIPS

## HELPS WITH

- Pancreas
- Spleen
- Lymph system
- Immune system
- Digestive system

## HOW

Gently bite your lips or move them in and out as though you are whistling, then smiling. Repeat 36 times.

You can also use the palm of either hand to massage your lips in a circle 36 times and then massage them in a circle in the opposite direction 36 times. Any way you would like to exercise your lips is helpful. Chant the sound "whooo."

### How Long
One to three minutes

### How Often
As needed

### Best Time
Anytime

---

### Why
Your lips have energy points connecting to many of your body's systems, especially the pancreas and stomach, and stimulating your lips helps cleanse your organs and stimulate these systems.

# 15 MOUTH, INHALING AND EXHALING THROUGH

## HELPS WITH

- Detoxifying your entire body
- Cleansing your entire body
- Decreasing stress

## HOW

Inhale through your nose, taking about five seconds, and then exhale through your mouth as slowly as you comfortably can. Silently or softly chanting one of the previously-mentioned sounds while you are exhaling is even better. Chant the sound "seee."

### How Long
Two to three minutes

### How Often
As needed

### Best Time
In the morning after you get up and before you meditate

> ### Why
> The slower you inhale, the more oxygen you take in, creating more energy and helping your body to detoxify and cleanse itself better. When you exhale slowly, more energy reaches your parasympathetic nervous system, which helps you relax and also helps to detoxify and cleanse your body.

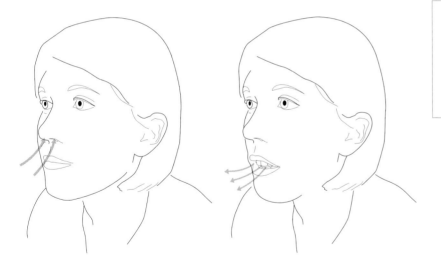

# 16 MOUTH, CORNERS OF

## HELPS WITH
- Constipation
- Digestive problems
- Diarrhea
- Gas

## HOW
Rub your hands until they're warm. Place your palms next to and below the corners of your mouth, and massage gently by moving your hands in a circular way 36 times (if helpful, puff out your cheeks for better access). Massage in the other direction 36 times, and then use your index and middle fingers to gently pat these areas for 30 seconds (Patting without massaging is also good). As you're doing this, chant the sound "whooo."

### How Long
One to two minutes

### How Often
As needed

### Best Time
Anytime

### Why
*The corners of your mouth have energy points connecting to your large intestines and digestive system.*

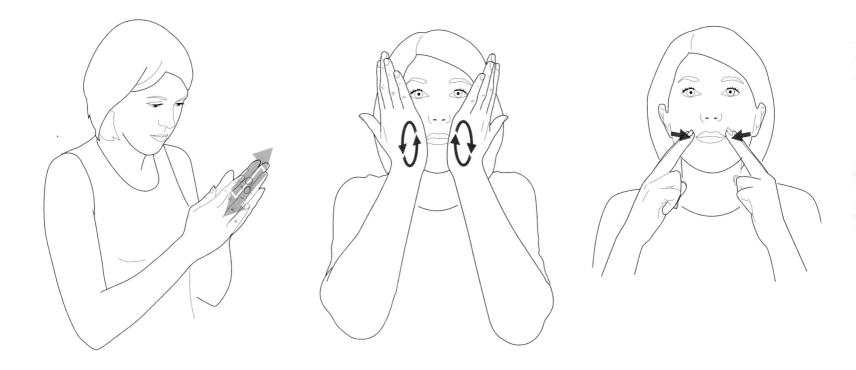

# 17 TEETH, TAPPING TOGETHER

## HELPS WITH

- Poor memory
- Alzheimer's Disease
- Brain clarity

- TMJ
- Acid reflux

## HOW

Open your jaw with your lips closed, and then tap your teeth together soundly so they make a single knocking sound. Open again and repeat 24 times to complete a set; you can do as many sets as you want. (This should not put any undue pressure on your teeth and should not hurt.)

**How Long**
One minute

**How Often**
As needed

**Best Time**
Anytime

*Why*

*Your teeth have nerves that connect to your brain, and this exercise stimulates and balances the energy in your brain, teeth, and gums. It also creates saliva, which is good for your esophagus and stomach.*

# 18 TEETH, BITING TOGETHER

## HELPS WITH

- Preventing life-force energy loss
- Achieving longevity
- Promoting bladder health
- Strengthening your prostate

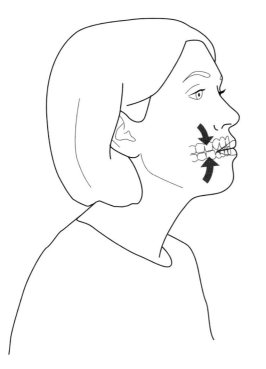

## HOW

When you urinate, bite your teeth together firmly (but not tightly).

### How Long

While you are urinating

### How Often

Whenever you urinate

### Why

Most of your energy is stored in your lower dantian, which is the energy center that is deep in behind your navel and connects to your kidneys. When you urinate you lose some of the energy from your kidneys. When you bite your teeth together firmly, you push the energy from your lower dantian to your middle dantian (in your heart area), and this action helps prevent energy loss, promoting the health of your bladder. If you are a man, it strengthens your prostate.

Biting your teeth while you're urinating automatically strengthens the muscles near your bladder and prostate and improves energy flow.

# 19 TONGUE

## HELPS WITH

- Heartburn
- Acid reflux
- Recovery from heart attack
- Loss of taste and smell

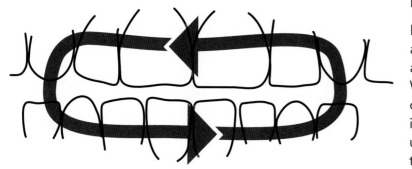

**HOW**

Open your jaw a little, close your lips, and put the tip of your tongue behind the center of your upper front teeth. Slide your tongue to the right side so it touches the back of all your upper teeth on that side. When you get to the end of that side, move your tongue down to the back of your teeth on the bottom of the same side.

Now slide your tongue around to touch the back of all your teeth on the bottom. When it gets to the last tooth on the far left side, move it up to the back of your upper teeth on that side and then back to the center of your front teeth, creating a complete circle.

Do this first to the right 36 times and then to the left 36 times at a comfortable pace. If you have time, you can follow the same procedure for the outside of your teeth too.

It is also good to swallow the saliva this exercise produces and visualize it going all the way down to your lower dantian, which is deep in behind your navel.

### How Long
However long it takes to do this 36 times in each direction

### How Often
As needed

### Best Time
Morning, noon, or anytime

---

**Why**

*Your tongue has energy points connecting to your lungs and to your heart—especially to your heart—and saliva created this way is good for helping with digestive issues.*

# 20 CHIN

## HELPS WITH

- Bladder infections
- Reproductive organ problems
- Menstrual period abnormalities
- Testicle infections (not STDs)

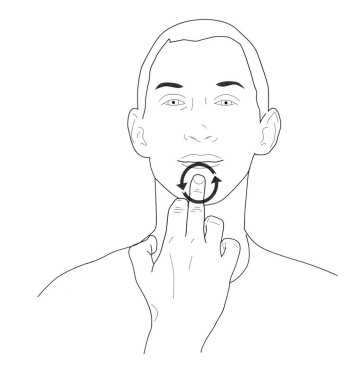

## HOW

Place the tip of your middle finger on the "ditch" that forms between your lower lip and your chin. Massage by holding your finger on this spot and gently moving it in a circle 36 times in one direction, then in a circle 36 times the other direction. Chant the sound "chueee."

### How Long
One minute

### How Often
Three times a day or as needed

---

*Why*
*Massaging your chin stimulates energy points that connect to your bladder and reproductive organs.*

# 21 FACE

## HELPS WITH
- Facial wrinkles
- Facial pain and numbness
- Headaches
- Dizziness/vertigo

## HOW
Rub your hands until they are warm. Place the index and middle fingers of your hands near the bottom of each side of your nose. Move them up the sides of your nose and over the bridge of your nose onto your forehead.

Now place all of your fingers on your forehead and gently but firmly move them outward, down over your temples, and down to your chin. Repeat several times. Chant the sound "kerrr."

### How Long
One to three minutes

### How Often
As needed

### Best Time
Anytime

### Why
*Your face has many energy points and nerves that connect to your brain, and massaging your face in this way restores balance in your brain and promotes health of your facial skin and nerves. Also, because your face has many energy points connecting to all your internal organs, this simple exercise is good for general health.*

*An interesting note: If you have a significant health challenge in your body, it usually shows up on your face. By doing this exercise you can help with those health challenges.*

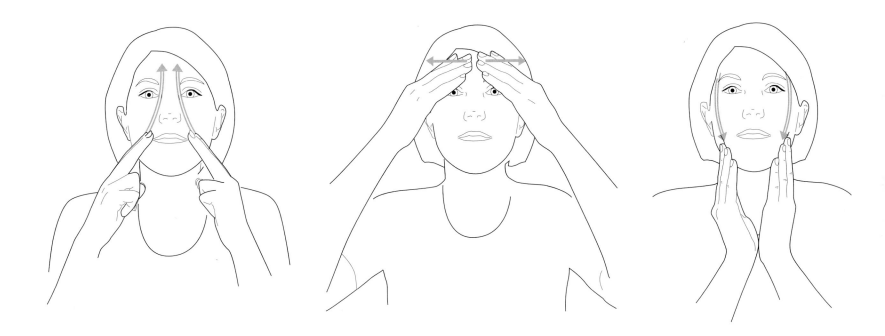

# 22 EARS, MASSAGING

## HELPS WITH

- Opening blockages in your organs
- Increasing mental clarity
- Increasing life-force energy
- Balancing the energy for your entire body
- Hearing problems

## HOW

Massage your entire ear from the top down to the lobe. Then pull down your lobe and hold it for three seconds. Release and repeat the entire exercise nine times. Do both ears simultaneously. Chant the sound "chueee."

### How Long
One minute

### How Often
As needed

### Best Time
Anytime

### Why

*This is one of the most simple and effective exercises you can do for stimulating energy in your body and opening blockages in your organs, because your ears have acupuncture points connecting to all the parts of your body. Massaging your ears is like giving your whole body a good tune-up.*

*If there is an abnormal feeling or pain in a particular part of your ear, it generally means there is an energy blockage in the relative part of your body. Keep massaging that spot until the abnormal feeling or pain disappears, indicating that the part of your body relative to the ear/s is healed, and the energy blockage is gone. The time this takes may vary.*

*(Having a sore spot on your ear, indicating an energy blockage, does not mean you have a serious problem in that organ. We all get energy blockages all the time, and most of the time they do move on.)*

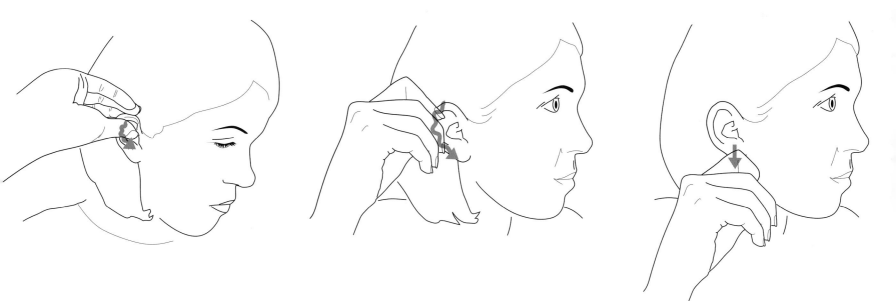

# 23 EARS, IN FRONT OF

## HELPS WITH

- Ear infections or any problems relating to ears
- Ringing in ears
- Deafness

## HOW

When you open your mouth and drop your jaw, you can feel a slight indentation right in front of your ear. Close your mouth and use your index fingers to massage these points by moving your fingers up and down slightly with pressure that is gentle to firm. Chant the sound "kerrr."

### How Long
One to three minutes

### How Often
As needed

### Best Time
Anytime

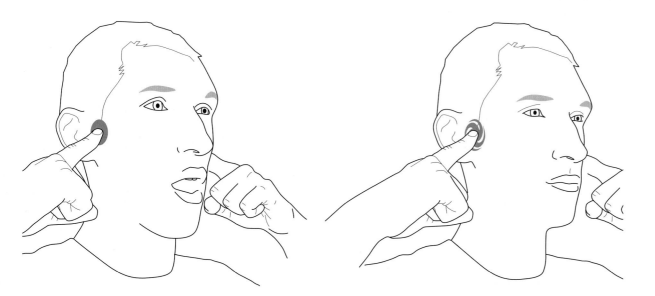

### Why
These points connect to your nervous system, and massaging here stimulates nerves that connect to energy channels in your ears.

# 24 EARS, IN FRONT OF AND BEHIND

## HELPS WITH
- Ringing in ears
- Hearing loss
- Ear infection
- Facial pain

## HOW
Spread your index and middle fingers apart, placing your index fingers on the bone behind each ear and your middle fingers on the bone in front of each ear. Massage in front of and behind your ears 36 times at two-second intervals by moving your hands up and down starting below your earlobes and moving up to the tops of your ears. Chant the sound "sheee."

### How Long
However long it takes

### How Often
Two times a day or more

### Best Time
Morning and evening or any time

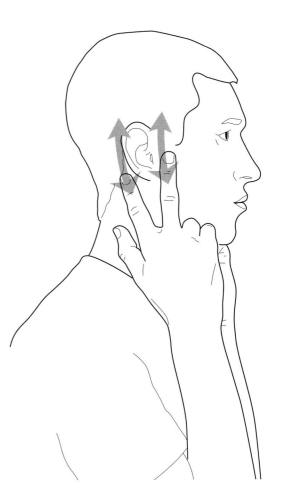

### Why
*Massaging this way can help enhance the circulation of energy in your ears, which also affects nerves in your face.*

# 25 EARS, CARTILAGE OF

## HELPS WITH
- Ringing in ears
- Hearing loss
- Balance (inner ear)

**HOW**

Use your middle fingers to press the protruding soft cartilage in front of your ears into your ears until you cannot hear anything. Hold this position for five seconds and then release your fingers quickly. Wait three seconds and repeat. This will be even more effective if you end the exercise by pulling down your earlobes and holding them for three seconds each time.

You can also do this while chanting: Inhale while your ears are open. Then, as you press the cartilage into your ears and close out all sound, exhale while chanting "chueee."

*How Long*
Three to five minutes

*How Often*
Two to three times a day, or more

*Best Time*
Anytime

*Why*
This exercise affects many energy points connecting to your hearing system and helps pop open energy blockages in your ear.

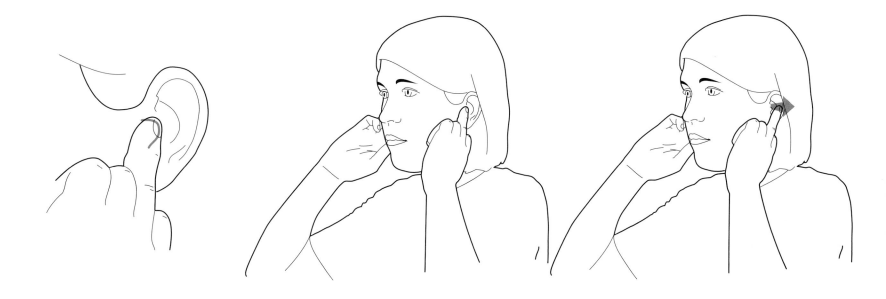

# 26 EARS, COVERING

## HELPS WITH

- Poor memory
- Hearing loss
- Strokes
- Insomnia

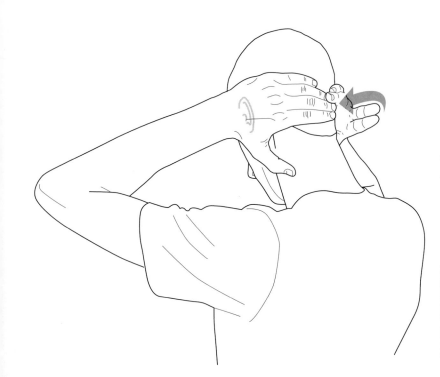

**HOW**

Cover your ears completely with your palms, not allowing in any air. Overlap your fingers on the back of your head, where your spine goes into your skull, with your right fingers on top.

Tap the back of your left index and middle fingers with your right index and middle fingers three times. Reverse your hand positions and place your right hand fingers on the base of your head, using your left index and middle fingers to tap the back of your right fingers three times. Repeat this between left and right eight times.

While you are doing the tapping, you will hear the sound vibrating in your ears like a drum being beaten. Chant the sound "chueee."

### How Long
One minute

### How Often
As needed

### Best Time
Morning or anytime

> **Why**
> The vibration created in this way helps open up the energy channels in your ears and brain that are directly connected to hearing. It is also helpful for reducing the stress in your brain and for helping you sleep.

# 27 THROAT, SIDES OF

## HELPS WITH
- Sore throat
- Hoarse voice
- Loss of voice

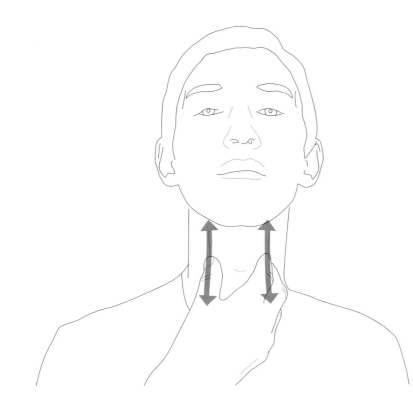

**HOW**
Use either hand or both hands to massage your throat by putting two fingers or a finger and a thumb on both sides of and above your Adam's apple and gently but firmly massaging down to your collarbone. Repeat many times a day. Chant the sound "sheee."

*How Long*
Two to ten minutes

*How Often*
Two to three times a day or more if needed

*Best Time*
Anytime

*Why*
A lot of energy channels run through this area. Massaging can help strengthen circulation of energy here.

# 28 NECK

## HELPS WITH

- Stress
- Neck pain
- Dizziness/vertigo
- Motion sickness
- Headaches
- Mental clarity

**HOW**

Sit or stand straight. Stretch your neck forward, move your chin down, and then tuck it back toward your chest. Now guide your chin up your chest until your head is back at the starting point. This is done in a continuous circular motion and should only take a few seconds. Chant the sound "kerrr."

*How Long*
One minute

*How Often*
As needed

*Best Time*
Anytime

*Why*

A major and wide energy channel comes up your spine and forms a narrow passage at the top of your shoulders where your neck starts. Keeping this channel open balances energy in your neck, helps relieve stress buildup, tense shoulders, headaches, and blocked flow of energy up into your brain.

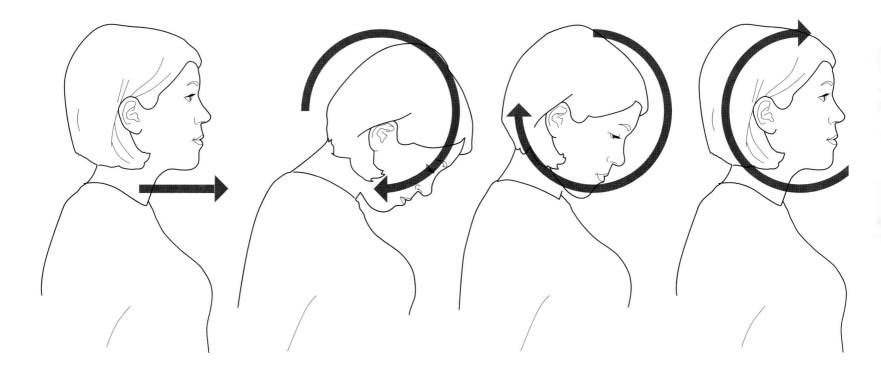

# 29 ARMS, RAISING

## HELPS WITH

- Congestion in your lungs and chest
- Coughing
- Runny nose
- Nose bleeds

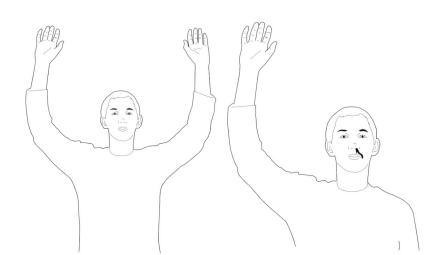

## HOW

Open your fingers and hold your hands above your head, making sure your elbows are above your shoulders. For lung problems holding both hands above your head is most effective; if you are engaged in an activity, holding up one hand is still helpful. Chant the sound "ceee."

For a nosebleed: If blood is coming out from your right nostril, raise your left hand. If blood is coming out from your left nostril, raise your right hand. If blood is coming out from both nostrils, raise both hands.

### *How Long*
One minute or as needed

### *How Often*
As needed

### *Best Time*
Anytime

---

### *Why*

*Holding your hands and arms above your head opens up a strong flow of energy through your lungs, large intestine, heart, and other meridians which start or end in your hands. It is especially good for your lungs.*

*This helps when you have a bloody nose because the left side of your brain affects the right side of your body, and the right side of your brain affects the left side of your body. When you raise your hands above your head, you create a pressure which forces the energy back to its own channels, and your body heals.*

# 30 ARMS, CUPPING

## HELPS WITH

- Breathing problems
- Runny nose
- Sinus problems
- Pneumonia

- Asthma
- Coughing
- Congestion in your lungs and chest

## HOW

Open your left hand and extend your arm with your palm facing up. Hold your right hand like a cup, as if it were holding water. Firmly pat (cup) the inside of your left arm every couple of inches from your shoulder down to your wrist. Continue for one minute and then repeat on your other arm. Chant the sound "seee."

### How Long
One minute per arm

### How Often
As needed

### Best Time
Morning or anytime

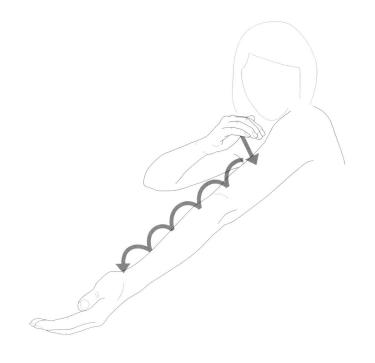

> ### Why
> All your lung and heart channels are arranged on the inside of your arms. Cupping helps open up blockages and stimulates energy flow.

# 31 ARMS, SWINGING

## HELPS WITH

- Scoliosis
- Aches and pains in your spine
- Spine degeneration
- Enhancing energy circulation

## HOW

Stand with your feet a little wider apart than your shoulders and look straight ahead. Keeping your hips stationary, raise your elbows to shoulder height. Keep your arms in front of you and parallel to the ground, your palms facing down, and your fingers pointing toward each other.

Swing your arms briskly from side to side eight times as you continue to keep your hips stationary and your head looking forward. Then, keeping your arms in the same position, lower them to waist level and again swing them eight times.

### How Long
One minute

### How Often
As needed

### Best Time
Anytime

### Why

*Your spine is very important and has lot of energy channels and nerve systems running through it. Keeping the channels open along your spine helps keep all the energy channels in your body open.*

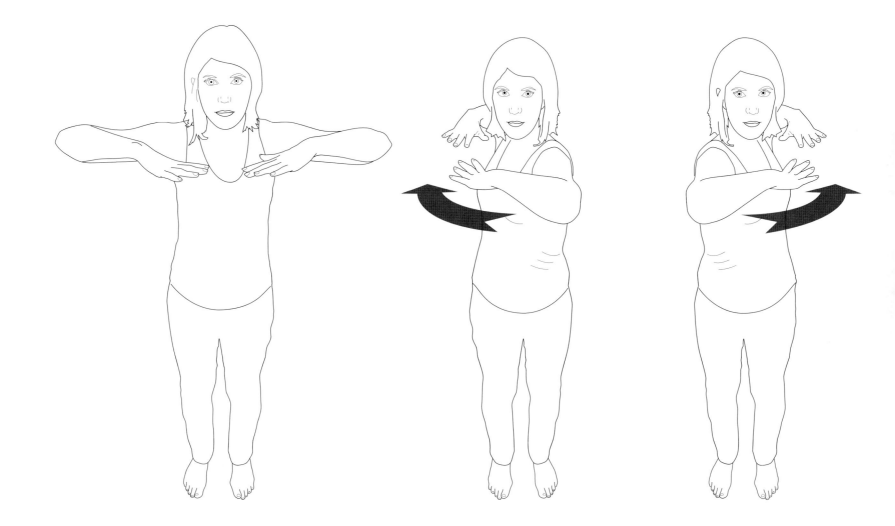

# 32 ELBOWS, MASSAGING

## HELPS WITH

- Pain anywhere in your arm
- Neuropathy
- Stomach pain
- Diarrhea

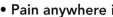

## HOW

Hold your left arm at a 90-degree angle with your forearm in front of your body and parallel to the floor. With your right hand, massage the spot between your forearm and your upper arm where the crease of skin ends (about an inch in from your elbow bone). Use your thumb to press deeply just until you start to feel some pain, then massage back and forth from side to side. Chant the sound "seee." Switch arms and repeat.

**Note:** Women who are pregnant or having a period should not massage this point because it might cause discomfort.

### How Long
Two minutes on each hand

### How Often
As needed

### Best Time
Anytime

> ### Why
> This point belongs to the large intestine channels and also has strong connections to your nervous system.

# 33 ELBOWS, CUPPING

## HELPS WITH

- Constipation
- Skin rashes
- Eye pain
- Thyroid conditions
- Liver problems
- Lymph system stimulation

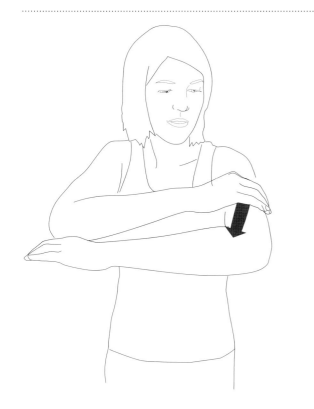

## HOW

Hold your left arm at a 90-degree angle with your forearm in front of your body and parallel to the floor. Hold your right hand like a cup, as if it were holding water. Gently but crisply pat (cup) the area on the top of your forearm that is one inch down from your elbow. Do this repeatedly.

### How Long
Two minutes on each arm

### How Often
Three times a day or more

### Best Time
5:00 a.m. to 7:00 a.m. or anytime

### Why
*This point connects to the large intestine channel and has strong connections to your liver and lymph systems.*

# 34 FOREARMS

## HELPS WITH

- Heart and chest pain
- Insomnia
- Stroke

- Irregular heartbeat
- Lymph system stimulation
- Immune system stimulation

## HOW

Find the first line at the bottom of your left palm. About two inches from this line (toward your elbow) there is a point located right in the middle of your forearm between two tendons (it may be sore). Massage this point firmly with your thumb and chant the sound "kerrr." Repeat on your other arm.

### How Long
One to two minutes per arm

### How Often
As often as you want

### Best Time
Anytime

### Why
This is an important energy point in your body which greatly affects your heart channel and lymph and immune systems. Massaging here strengthens circulation in your heart, which can improve insomnia.

# 35 WRISTS

## HELPS WITH

- Reproductive organ problems
- Heart issues, such as blocked arteries, blood pressure problems, and recovery from a heart attack or heart surgery

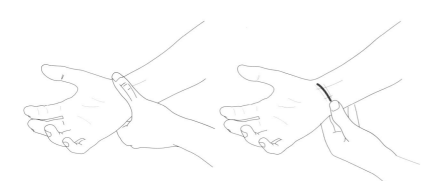

### Why

This area has many energy points connecting directly to your heart and reproductive organs. Sometimes when you massage deeply here and find discomfort in a spot, you will know there is a specific energy blockage that needs attention. Massage that spot until the pain is gone.

## HOW

Use the thumb on one hand to massage the area that is on the inside of the wrist of your other hand between the first and second line where the wrist bends. Massage gently but firmly from one side to the other. Repeat with the other hand.

Then let your hands fall forward limply, and rotate them in a circle either way. Do both hands at the same time—first one way and then the other. Chant the sound "chueee."

### How Long
Five to ten minutes

### How Often
As often as you want

### Best Time
Anytime

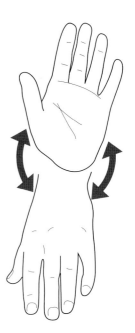

# 36 HANDS, "V" SPOT ON

## HELPS WITH

- Headaches
- Heart pain
- Stomach pain
- High blood pressure
- Fever
- Eye fatigue

## HOW

Use your right thumb to massage the spot in the "V" on the back of your left hand an inch into the "web" where the bones of your thumb and index finger meet. Switch hands and repeat. Chant the sound "seee."

**Note:** Women who are pregnant or having a period should not massage this point because it might cause discomfort.

### How Long
One to two minutes

### How Often
Three or more times a day

### Best Time
Anytime

### Why
This point is on the large intestine channel that runs from your hand to your head. Massaging here can help activate the energy along the entire channel, including your head, as well as the organs influenced by this channel.

# 37 HANDS, BACK OF

## HELPS WITH

• Aging spots

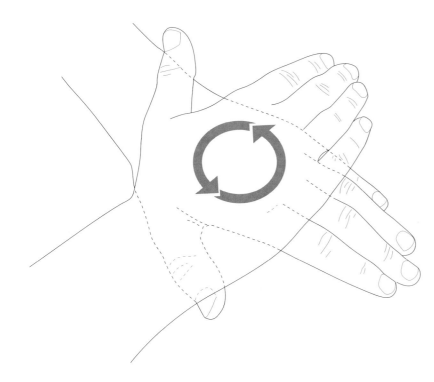

## HOW

Use the palm of your right hand to massage the back of your left hand using a circular movement. Massaging either direction is fine, and massaging different directions at different times is fine too. Do this for at least one minute. While you are massaging your hand, repeat this message from your heart: "All my channels are open; the aging spots in my body are completely gone." Repeat using the palm of your left hand to massage the back of your right hand. Chant the sound "seee."

### How Long
One to three minutes per hand

### How Often
As needed

### Best Time
Morning or anytime

### Why
*The backs of your hands are the areas where the qi of yin and yang for the skin meet. Massaging here helps break up blockages that lead to aging spots anywhere on your skin.*

# 38 HANDS, BACK AND INDEX FINGER SIDE OF

## HELPS WITH
- **Any blockages in your body**
- **Aches and pains anywhere in your body**

## HOW
Use your thumb to massage along the side of the bone that runs from the knuckle at the base of your index finger about an inch and one-half toward your wrist.

### How Long
Two minutes on each hand

### How Often
As needed

### Best Time
Anytime

> ### Why
> *Massaging here stimulates energy in your organs and throughout your body. This is a good, simple exercise you can practice just about anywhere.*

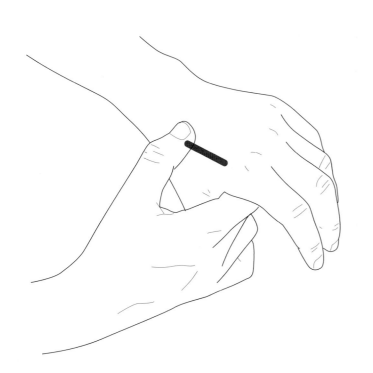

# 39 HANDS, TWO SPOTS ON BACK OF

## HELPS WITH

- Sore throat
- Infection or any other problems in your throat

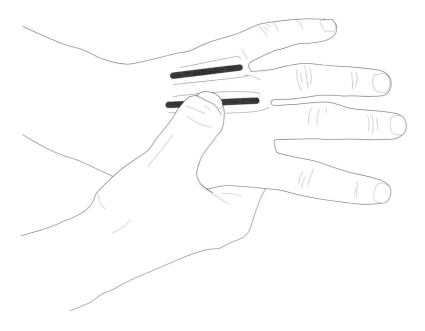

## HOW

Use your right thumb to massage an inch or two below the knuckles on the back of your hand in two spots: between the bones coming down from your middle finger and your ring finger (this area will probably be sore) and between the bones coming down from your ring finger and your little finger. Repeat with the other hand.

### How Long
One minute per hand

### How Often
As often as you want

### Best Time
Anytime

### Why
These areas have energy channels connecting directly to your neck, head, and throat.

**Note:** This exercise is especially good for teachers and other people who use their voices a lot.

# 40 PALMS, "PALMING" WITH

## HELPS WITH

- Pain
- Swelling
- Eye problems
- Arthritis

## HOW

Rub your hands together until they are very warm, and apply the middle of one or both palms on the area where you or your friend have pain. While your hand(s) is on that area, repeatedly send a silent healing message from your heart, such as: "The pain is gone—completely healed." This is not only good for pain, but also for swelling, eye problems, arthritis, etc.

If you can visualize light coming out of your palm(s) and going into the area that needs healing energy, it will be even better. Chant the sound "kerrr."

### How Long
Three to five minutes or longer as needed

### How Often
As needed

### Best Time
Anytime

### Why
*In the middle of your palms there is a very powerful healing energy center; when you rub your hands together until they are warm, you activate this energy. When you put your palm on a specific area, it activates the energy in that area. Using your palms in this way can help maintain health and can help heal in areas where you have specific problems. Many minor problems can be helped by doing this.*

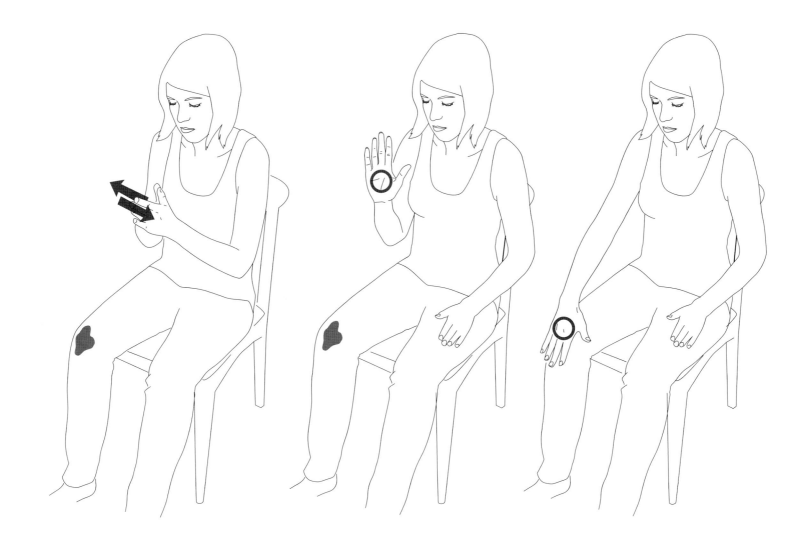

# 41 PALMS, MASSAGE

## HELPS WITH

- Menstrual and muscle cramps
- Heart problems
- Stroke recovery
- High blood pressure
- High cholesterol

## HOW

Curve your middle finger, touch your palm, and note the spot. Then firmly massage that spot with the thumb of your other hand. If you have trouble finding the spot, just massage the area in your palm between the bones of your index and middle fingers.

### How Long

Two minutes on each hand

### How Often

A couple times a day to help heal your heart and as often as feels good for cramps

### Best Time

Anytime

### Why

This point has a strong connection to your heart and to your brain. Massaging here can help menstrual and muscle cramps.

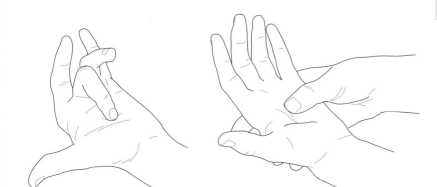

# 42 PALM AND FINGER

## HELPS WITH
- Healing cancers
- Cleansing your lymph system
- Building your immune system

## HOW
Curve your ring finger naturally until the tip touches your palm. Hold it there gently and chant the sound "ceee."

### How Long
As long as you can. This posture is very convenient to do anywhere, both hands at once or one hand at a time, and you do not need to do any meditation.

### How Often
As needed

### Best Time
Anytime

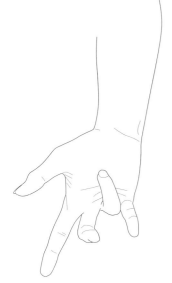

> ### Why
> The energy system that helps many of your bodily functions, especially the cleansing of waste and toxins, is located where your ring finger touches your palm. Simply stimulating this point by holding your finger on it helps stimulate the energy.

# 43 FINGER, INDEX AND THUMB

## HELPS WITH

- Warming cold hands and feet
- Feeling drained by people or places

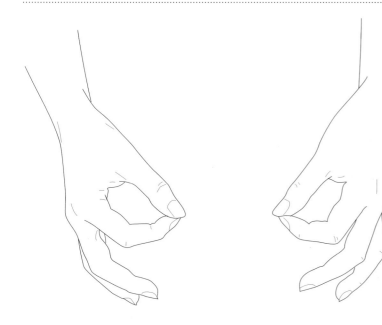

## HOW

Gently connect the tip of your index finger with the tip of your thumb, making a circle. You can do this with two hands or one. If you choose, you can put your hand(s) into your pocket(s) so that nobody will see what you are doing. Chant the sound "kerrr."

### How Long
As long as you want

### How Often
As needed

### Best Time
Whenever you need to

### Why

*Holding your finger and thumb in this position helps keep your life-force energy inside your body longer, which can help your hands and feet stay warm. Sometimes, with certain places or certain people, you may feel that your energy gets drained. This is especially true if you are sick or run down. By holding your fingers in this position, you only allow energy to come into your body, not to drain out.*

# 44 FINGERS, INDEX AND RING

## HELPS WITH
- **Diabetes**
- **High or low blood sugar**

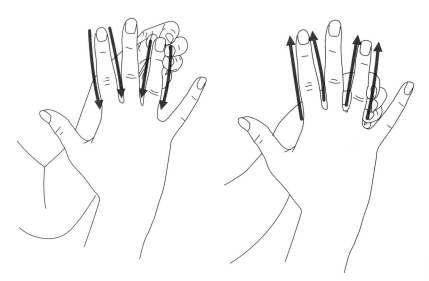

## HOW
Hold up your left hand and massage the sides of your index and your ring fingers.

For high blood sugar, grasp the sides of your finger at the tip and massage or firmly stroke down to the base. For low blood sugar, do just the opposite, massaging from base to tip. While you are doing this, repeat a message from your heart: "All my channels are open; my blood sugar is down to normal," or "All my channels are open, my blood sugar is up to normal." Repeat with your other hand. You may do both fingers or alternate between your index and your ring finger, whichever feels best to you. Chant the sound "seee."

### How Long
At least two minutes per hand

### How Often
As needed

### Best Time
Morning, late afternoon, or anytime

> ## Why
> *Diabetes is connected to your digestive system and to the balance of your endocrine system. Your index fingers have a direct relationship with your digestive system, and your ring fingers have the energy point that is directly connected to your endocrine system. This massage helps balance these channels and organ systems, helps prevent energy blockages in these areas, and helps strengthen your immune system.*

# 45 FINGER, INDEX AND THUMB

## HELPS WITH
• Injuries to your spine
• Energy blockages along your spine

## HOW
Interlock your fingers until the webbing between the fingers of each hand touches, then pull your hands apart. Repeat over and over. The important energetic stimulation happens when the webbing touches as your fingers interlock. This can be done quickly or slowly. Chant the sound "chueee."

## How Long
One to three minutes

## How Often
As often as you want

## Best Time
Anytime

## Why
*The vibration from this movement stimulates the energy along your spine, helping it to flow smoothly.*

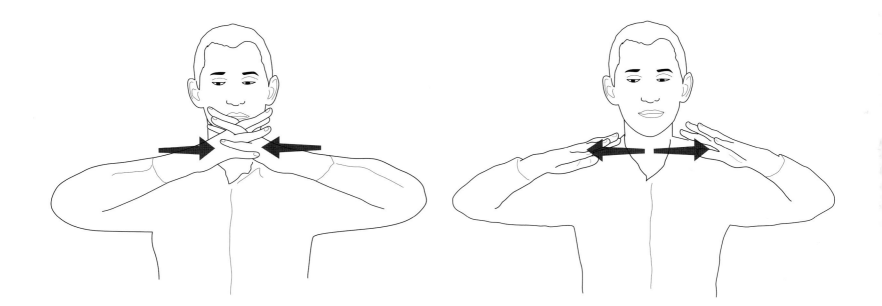

# 46 FINGERS, LITTLE AND MIDDLE

## HELPS WITH
- **High blood pressure**
- **Low blood pressure**

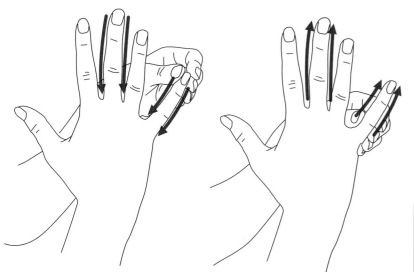

## HOW
Hold up your left hand and massage the sides of your middle and little fingers.

For high blood pressure, grasp the sides of your finger at the tip and massage or firmly stroke down to the base. For low blood pressure, do just the opposite, massaging or stroking upward. While you are doing this, repeat a message from your heart: "All my channels are open; my blood pressure is down to normal," or "All my channels are open; my blood pressure is up to normal."

Repeat with the other hand. Massage your middle finger, your little finger, or both fingers. Chant the sound "kerrr."

### How Long
One to three minutes on each finger

### How Often
As needed

### Best Time
Noon, late afternoon, or anytime

> **Why**
> The heart channels are located in these two fingers, and blood pressure has a lot to do with your heart and your liver.

# 47 FINGERS, TAPPING

## HELPS WITH
- **Asthma**
- **Stroke**
- **Memory**

## HOW
Holding your hands as if you were playing a piano, using all ten fingers simultaneously, tap a hard flat surface such as a table (not too gently and not too hard). Chant the sound "kerrr."

### How Long
One to three minutes

### How Often
As often as you want

### Best Time
Anytime

### Why
*The tips of your fingers have important energy points connecting to your brain and to your heart.*

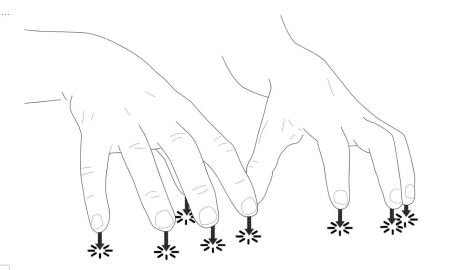

# 48 SPINE

## HELPS WITH

- Headaches
- Colds
- Fever
- Neck and shoulder pain

## HOW

Use either hand to massage the area on both sides of C7, which is the protruding bone toward the top of your spine at the height of the top of your shoulders. Squeeze the skin and hold it tightly for three seconds. Release the muscle and then hold it tightly again for three seconds and let go. Repeat the squeeze-and-release motion nine times.

**Note:** This may feel awkward or somewhat uncomfortable.

### How Long
Two to three minutes

### How Often
Three times a day or as needed

### Best Time
Anytime

---

### Why

C7 is one of the most important energy points in your body. It connects your head and your torso and is often the first area where energy flow gets constricted. A lot of problems can be healed by opening the channel in this area.

---

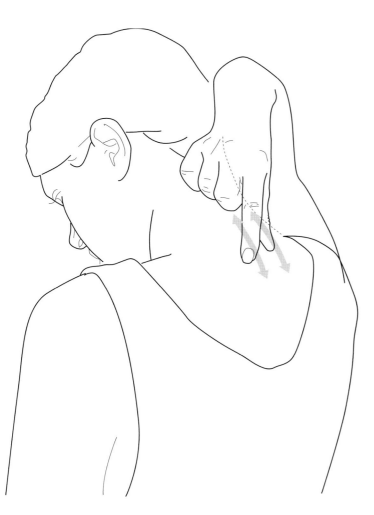

# 49 TORSO, BOUNCING

## HELPS WITH

- Cleansing your lymph system
- Strengthening your immune system
- Healing your whole spine
- Balancing your whole body
- Relieving shoulder pain

## HOW

This is a two-part exercise:

1. Stand with your feet a little more than shoulder-width apart and parallel to each other. Bring your focus to your knees and bounce your body up and down, bending your knees a few inches each time you bounce and keeping your feet on the floor. While you are bouncing, relax your shoulders and torso and keep your spine straight, but relaxed.

2. Now put your hands straight up above your head and continue to bounce. As your body moves up and down, don't try to control your hands. Allow them to bend at the wrist and flop limply. Doing this helps open the channels in your body faster.

### How Long
One to three minutes or longer

### How Often
As needed

### Best Time
Morning or anytime

## Why

*Bouncing grounds your energy in your lower torso and helps your lymph and immune systems. Holding your arms above your head is good because it opens up the energy channels in your lungs. A lot of important energy points are located in your wrists and connect to your heart, lungs, and reproductive organs. Bouncing like this can help open these energy points faster.*

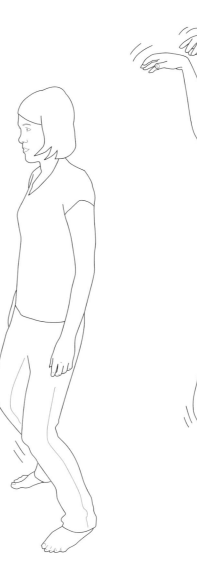

# 50 TORSO, SIDES

## HELPS WITH

- Coughing
- Pneumonia
- Breast infection
- Lung and breast lumps
- Pancreas problems

## HOW

Hold up your left arm to at least shoulder height. Form your right hand into a cup, as though it were holding water, and gently but firmly pat (cup) your arm every couple of inches down the side of your torso from directly under your armpit to the bottom of your ribcage (this should not hurt). Do this several times slowly or quickly. Repeat on your right side.

### How Long

One minute per side

### How Often

Three times a day or as needed

### Best Time

In early morning or anytime

> ### Why
> This area contains your pancreas channel and has energy points that connect to your lungs and to your breasts.

# 51 CHEST

## HELPS WITH

- Shortness of breath
- Coughing
- Congestion and pain in your heart or chest
- Increasing milk supply in new mothers
- Depression

**HOW**
Use your middle finger to massage the point located right in the middle of your chest between your breasts. Massage it in a circular way either direction or both directions, gently but firmly.

*How Long*
One to three minutes

*How Often*
Two times a day or more if needed

*Best Time*
Anytime

*Why*
This energy point has a strong connection to your heart energy center and to your entire chest.

# 52 BREASTS (FOR FEMALES)

## HELPS WITH

- Hot flashes
- Irregular periods
- Blockages in your breasts
- Hormone imbalance
- Reproductive problems

## HOW

Rub your palms together until they are warm. Place the center of each palm on the corresponding nipple. Focusing on your heart the entire time, move your hands gently inward, down, and around in a circular motion 36 times, then in the opposite direction 36 times; with your hands in the same position, gently lift and hold your breasts while you take three gentle deep breaths.

### How Long

Two to three minutes

### How Often

Two times a day

### Best Time

Early morning and before going to bed

### Why

*Your breasts belong to your kidney energy system and have a strong connection to your reproductive organs.*

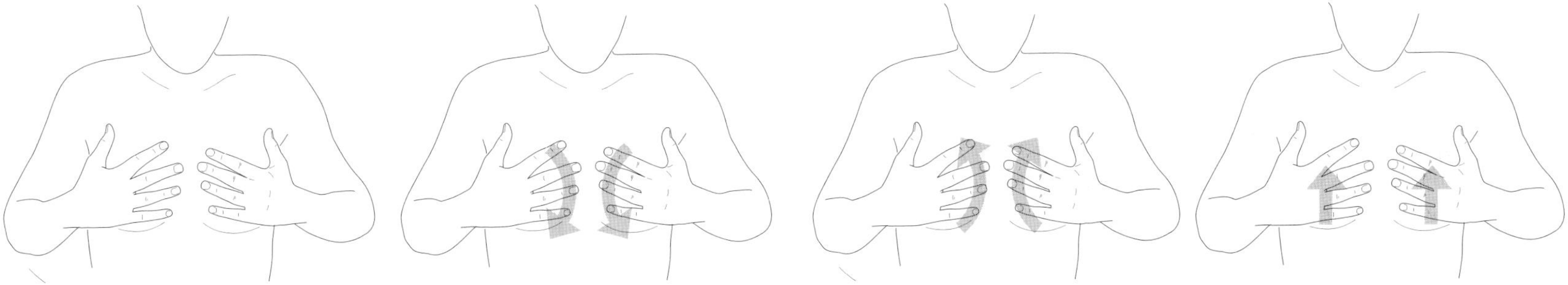

# 53 KIDNEYS

## HELPS WITH

- Kidney stones
- Kidney failure
- Kidney or life-force energy
- Low sexual energy
- Fatigue

## HOW

Hold your hands like cups, as if they were holding water, or hold them as empty fists with your thumbs and index fingers touching. Bend slightly forward and cup or pat the kidney area on your lower back. (If you cannot reach high enough, or are not sure exactly where your kidneys are, pat as high up your back as you can and visualize your kidneys right under where you are patting.)

### *How Long*
One to three minutes

### *How Often*
Three times at day or as needed

### *Best Time*
Anytime

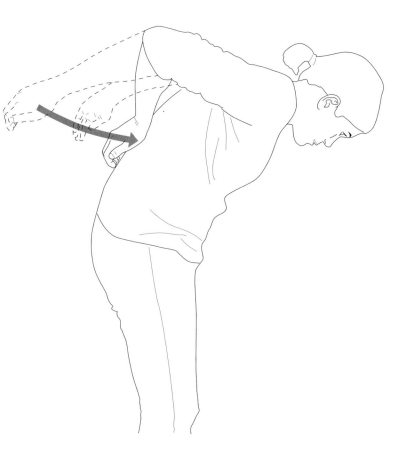

---

*Why*

*Kidney, or life-force, energy is the most important energy for your life. Any problems in your body start first with a weakness of kidney energy, so it is always important to keep that energy strong.*

# 54 STOMACH

## HELPS WITH
- **High blood pressure**
- **Nausea**
- **Vomiting**
- **Stomachache**
- **Insomnia**

### HOW
Massage the spot in the middle of your stomach, about four inches above your navel, with your middle finger. Massage gently, but firmly, in a circular way either direction. This spot may be a little tender.

### How Long
One to three minutes

### How Often
Once a day or more if needed

### Best Time
At noon or anytime

---

### Why
*This point connects with and enhances circulation in your stomach and other main energy channels.*

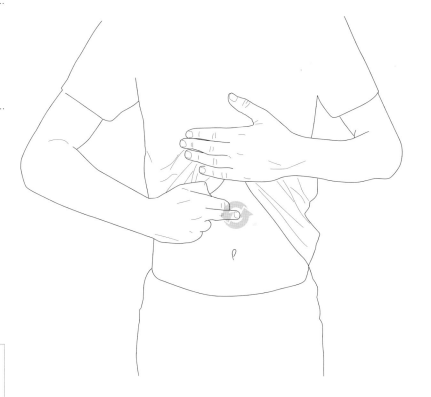

# 55 HIPS

## HELPS WITH

- Sciatic pain
- Numbness in your legs (legs "asleep")
- Neuropathy
- Damaged cartilage in hips and knees

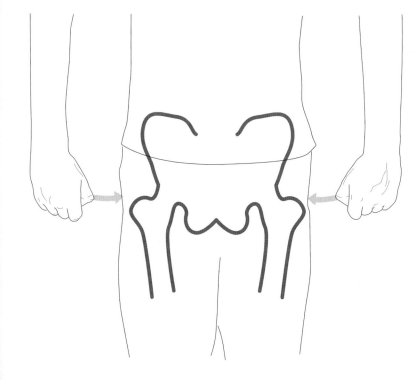

## HOW

This point is located a little behind your hip bone at about the same level as your pubic bone. Make a fist with both hands with your thumbs tucked inside, and tap the point in the hollow right behind your hip bones with your thumb or index finger knuckle as firmly as you can without discomfort.

### How Long
One to three minutes

### How Often
Three times a day or as needed

### Best Time
Anytime

---

### Why
*This point is a connection between the lower part of your body and your torso. Keeping it open is very important, especially if you sit a lot or have any problems in the lower part of your body.*

---

# 56 TAILBONE

## HELPS WITH

- Recovery from stroke
- Memory problems
- Enlarged prostate
- Irregular menstruation
- Life-force energy
- Reproductive organ problems
- Sexual functioning problems
- Kidney stones

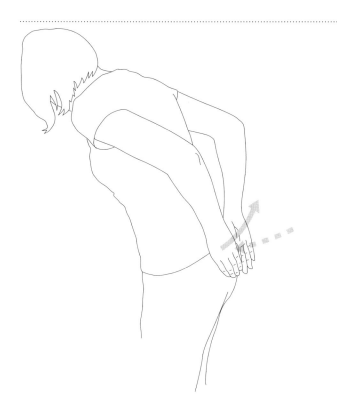

## HOW

Bend forward slightly and use both hands alternately to do one of the following:

1. Holding your hand like a cup, as though it were holding water, tap (cup) your tailbone and sacrum area as firmly as you can without discomfort.

2. With an open fist, touch the thumb and index finger of each hand together to make a circle; with this circle, tap your tailbone and sacrum area. Do this as firmly as you can without discomfort.

### How Long
One to three minutes each time

### How Often
Many times a day

### Best Time
Anytime

---

*Why*
*Your tailbone is considered an important gateway for life-force energy into your kidneys and connects to your brain and reproductive organs.*

# 57 TESTICLES

## HELPS WITH
- Prostate problems
- Low life-force energy
- Fatigue
- Testicle infections (not STDs)

**HOW**

While you are lying down, bend your legs, keeping your feet flat on the bed. Rub your palms together until they're warm. Place your right hand on your navel and your left hand directly on your testicles (skin to skin) and massage gently. Change hands and repeat.

**How Long**

Four to ten minutes

**How Often**

Two times a day

**Best Time**

Early morning and before going to bed at night

*Why*

*Your testicles are very important to the health of your male organs and to your life-force energy.*

# 58  KNEES

## HELPS WITH
- Hip pain
- Knee pain
- Sciatic pain
- Rib and chest pain

## HOW
Press your thumb or fingers in the spot just below your knee on the outside edge of your shin bone. Do one or both knees.

### How Long
Two minutes or more

### How Often
Two to three times a day

### Best Time
Anytime

### Why
This energy point is on your gallbladder channel, which goes through your knees and your sciatic area (lower back).

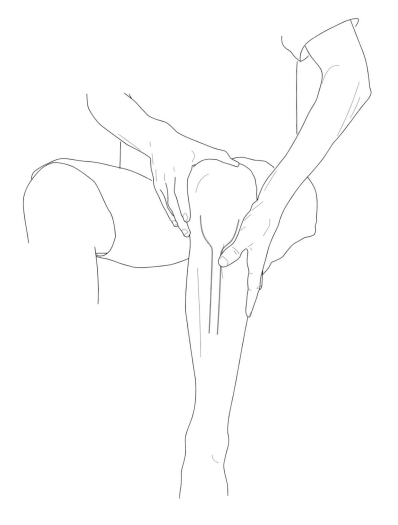

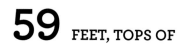

# 59 FEET, TOPS OF

## HELPS WITH
- Blockages in liver
- Insomnia
- Anger
- Urine leakage

## HOW
Massage the point on the top of your foot about two inches from the webbing that is between your big toe and your second toe—between the bones coming from those two toes.

### How Long
One to three minutes

### How Often
One or two times a day

### Best Time
Anytime

> ### Why
> Your liver channel is a major channel that connects to many areas of your body, and massaging this point stimulates all the areas along this channel.

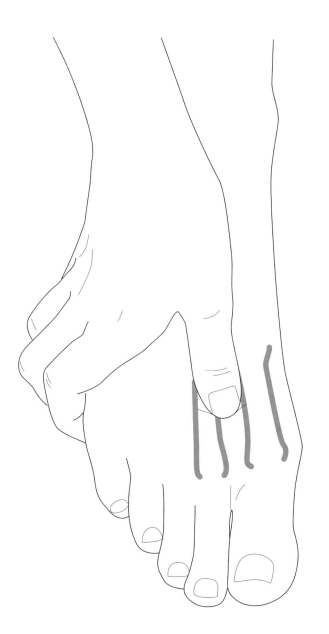

# 60 FEET, ARCHES

## HELPS WITH

• Balancing your whole body

## HOW

Massage the arch of your foot along the edge of the bone starting from the base of your big toe and moving to the end of the bone. Continuously massage, pushing the energy from the base of your big toe along your arch.

### How Long

Five minutes or more.

You can do both feet at the same time, if you like.

### How Often

Once a day or more if needed

### Best Time

Anytime

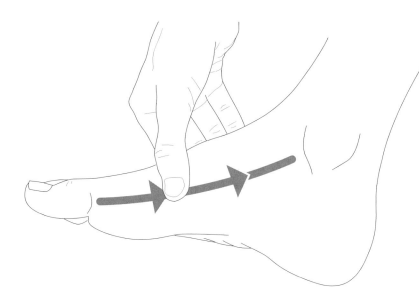

> ### Why
> This is another area that has many energy points; when you massage your foot this way, it stimulates the energy in your entire body. Massaging this area every day can also help reduce stress in your feet, especially when you stand for long periods of time.

# 61 FEET, BOTTOMS OF

## HELPS WITH

- Constipation
- Urination difficulty
- Colds
- Fever
- Low energy

## HOW

Massage the bottom of your foot on the point located down from the second and third toes where you see two lines meet. Do one foot and then the other.

## How Long

One to three minutes

## How Often

Once a day

## Best Time

Anytime

> ### Why
> This is one of the energy points in your body that is called a "longevity point." It belongs to the kidney energy channel and effects many other channels.

# 62 HEELS

## HELPS WITH
- Constipation
- Cold hands
- Cold feet

## HOW
Stand with your feet a little less than shoulder-width apart. Rise up onto the balls of your feet and then let your body drop back down to the ground.

**Note:** If you have lower back problems or you are pregnant, it would be best to skip this exercise. Doing this technique on a concrete floor with no shoes is not recommended.

### How Long
One to three minutes

### How Often
Anytime

### Best Time
Morning and/or late afternoon

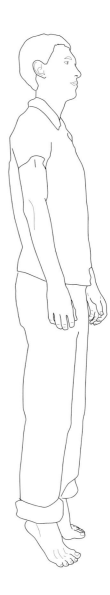

> ### Why
> *The vibration from this movement helps open channels in your spine, your kidneys, and your head.*

# 63 TOES, GRASPING WITH

## HELPS WITH
- Low energy
- Weight loss, for people who are overweight

## HOW
When you sit, with or without shoes, hold your toes as though you are grasping the ground.

### How Long
As long as you like

### How Often
Whenever you remember to do it

### Best Time
Anytime

### Why
*When you exercise your feet this way, you stimulate energy in all six important energy channels that support your brain and your body.*

**Note:** This is especially good for those who sit working at a desk for long hours.

# 64 TOES, GRASPING WITH THUMB AND FINGER

## HELPS WITH
• Quickly clearing numbness in a leg that is "asleep"

## HOW
Use your thumb and index finger to tightly grasp and pull the neck of your big toe on the leg that is numb.

### How Long
Hold one to two minutes

### How Often
As needed

### Why
This helps to open your pancreas channel, and helps clear the numbness.

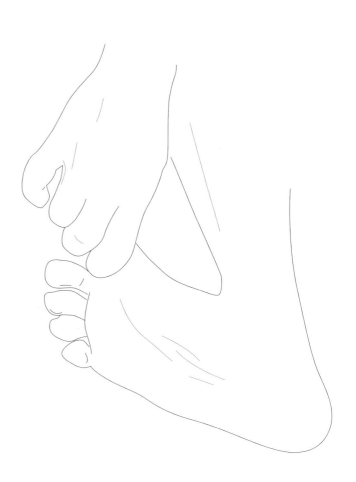

# Babies

# 65 HEAD

## HELPS WITH

- Calming emotions
- Preventing colds
- Increasing wisdom energy

## HOW

Put your palm on the soft part at the top of the baby's head and massage gently clockwise, visualizing golden light going into his or her brain.

### How Long

One to three minutes

### How Often

Two to three times a day, if possible

### Best Time

Anytime

### Why

The energy from your palm is passed on to the baby's brain, producing more calm, peace, and comfort and promoting healthy development of his or her brain.

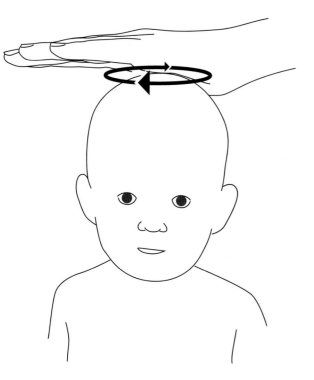

# 66 NOSE

## HELPS WITH
- **Heart and lung problems**
- **Dizziness/vertigo**

### HOW
Massage the point that is located right under the baby's nose on his or her upper lip. Use your middle finger to massage this area firmly in a circular way.

Now massage the spot on the baby's chest directly between his or her nipples.

### How Long
One to three minutes

### How Often
Two times or more

### Best Time
Anytime

### Why
*Massaging these two points stimulates the baby's brain, heart, and lungs.*

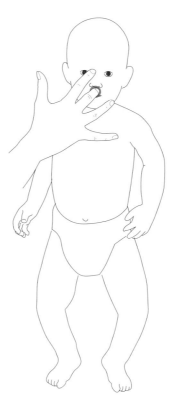

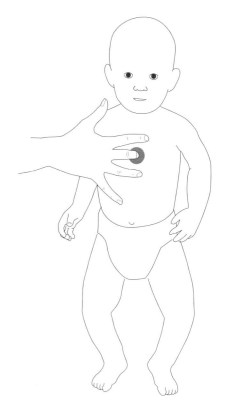

# 67 WRISTS

## HELPS WITH
- Calming emotions
- Clearing chest congestion
- Relieving digestive problems

### HOW
Rub either or both of the baby's hands at the bottom of his or her palms where the first line on the wrist appears. Massage the area up and down and back and forth.

### How Long
One to three minutes

### How Often
As needed

### Best Time
Anytime

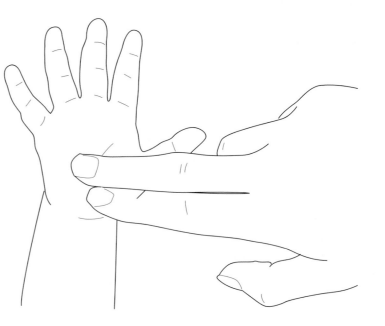

### Why
This part of the body has a direct connection to the baby's chest and stomach. He or she can feel comfortable and calmed when you massage here.

 **FINGERS**

## HELPS WITH

- Fever
- Emotional upset
- Development of the nervous system
- Anxiety and fear

### HOW
Massage the fingertips on the baby's left hand starting with the middle finger and then moving to the index finger, the ring finger, the thumb, and finally the little finger. Repeat on the baby's right hand.

### How Long
The longer the better

### How Often
A couple times a day or more if needed

### Best Time
Anytime

### Why
*The tips of the fingers connect directly to the heart and brain and massaging this way helps balance that energy.*

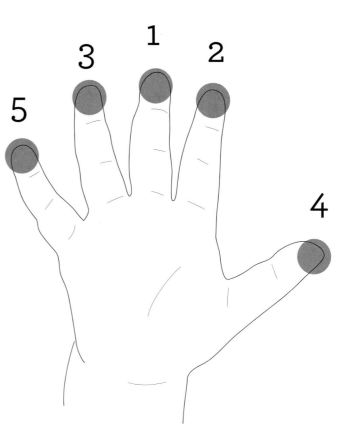

# 69 NAVEL

## HELPS WITH

- Constipation
- Vomiting
- Insomnia

- Strengthening the immune system

## HOW
Use your middle finger to very gently massage inside the baby's navel clockwise approximately 50 times, then counterclockwise approximately 50 times. Chant the sound "chueee."

### How Long
Two to three minutes

### How Often
One or two times a day, if needed

### Best Time
In the evening before the baby falls asleep

> **Why**
> The navel has a connection to the lower dantian, which is the vitality center. It also connects to the stomach, lymph system, immune system, and reproductive organs.

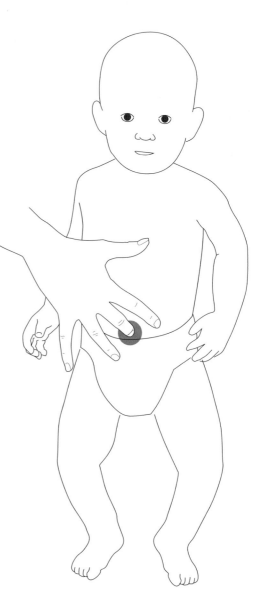

# 70 FEET

## HELPS WITH

- Enhancing energy circulation
- Strengthening the digestive system
- Strengthening the immune system
- Preventing and healing colds

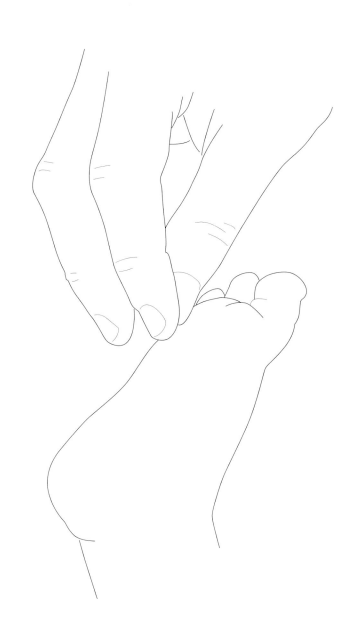

## HOW

Use your fingers to lightly tickle or massage the bottom of the baby's feet.

### How Long

One to three minutes

### How Often

A couple times a day or more

### Best Time

Anytime

### Why

*The bottoms of the feet have a lot of energy points connecting to the internal organs. When you tickle or massage the bottoms of a baby's feet, it helps to enhance the circulation of energy in his or her entire body.*

# 71 WRISTS

## HELPS WITH
- Diarrhea
- Balancing energy in the organs

## HOW
Use your thumb to massage back and forth across the baby's or child's wrist right under the crease where the hand and arm meet. Do the left wrist first, then the right. Chant the sound "whooo."

### How Long
Three minutes

### How Often
As needed

### Best Time
Anytime

> **Why**
> Many energy points are located here that connect directly to many important energy channels, including the digestive system channel.

# 72 STOMACH

## HELPS WITH
- **Stomach pain**
- **Cramps anywhere in the body**

## HOW
Use your thumbs to massage both sides of the baby's or child's stomach two inches down from and two inches to the sides of his or her navel. Do this gently and firmly in a circular way in either direction. Chant the sound "whooo."

### How Long
One to three minutes

### How Often
As needed

### Best Time
In the morning before breakfast or in the evening before bedtime

### Why
*These points connect to the stomach and gallbladder channels. Massaging here helps to balance energy in the stomach, gallbladder, and intestines.*

# Miscellaneous

# 73 SITTING ON HEELS (FOR PREGNANT WOMEN)

## HELPS WITH
- Helping the baby turn to get ready for delivery
- Opening up your sacrum and strengthening your life-force energy to ease delivery

### HOW
Bend your knees and sit right on your heels and calves with your knees apart. Put your hands in front of you to support your upper body. You can do this on the floor or on something soft, such as a bed.

### How Long
Thirty minutes

### How Often
Two times a day

### Best Time
Morning and evening

> ### Why
> This is an ideal technique for helping the baby turn to the right position for birth. If the baby is already in the right position, this posture is still very good for opening your kidney channel, which increases your overall energy; it gently opens your sacrum.

# 74 STANDING WITH KNEES BENT

## HELPS WITH
• Strengthening your kidney, or life-force, energy
• Losing weight, if weight loss is needed

### HOW
Stand with your feet parallel and a little more than shoulder-width apart. Bend your knees, keeping your spine straight.

For weight loss, bend your knees a little more.

### How Long
Ten to thirty minutes

### How Often
Once a day or as often as you like

### Best Time
Anytime

### Why
*Weak legs often suggest that kidney energy, or life-force energy, is weak. Weight gain can follow weak kidney energy. Standing in this position helps strengthen your legs and your life-force energy and can help you lose weight.*

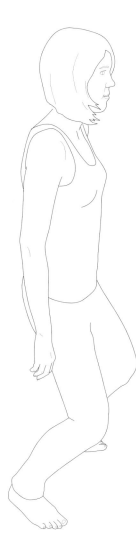

# 75 YIN-YANG WATER

## HELPS WITH

- Balancing your entire body
- Cleansing your liver
- Cleansing your pancreas
- Strengthening your digestive system

## HOW

Mix boiled water and cool water together in equal amounts and drink while still warm, adding a little honey if you'd like.

**Note:** Do not use the microwave for this.

### Best time to drink

Anytime, but best at the same time each day in order to create a habit

### Why

This is called "yin-yang healing water," and has been used by Chinese Taoists for overall health for thousands of years.

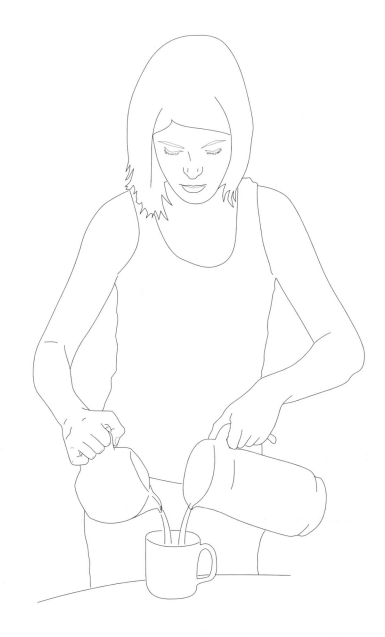

# 76 MOUTH, SMILING

## HELPS WITH
- Healing any blockages
- Stress
- Depression

## HOW
Take a deep breath, relax your body, and sink your consciousness into the light in your heart, putting a smile on your face. Focus on the particular part of your body where you have a challenge, and see your smile going into that part and the whole area filled with light. Give yourself a healing message—something like, "All the pain will be gone; I'm completely healed."

### How Long
Two to three minutes or as long as you like

### How Often
As often as you need

### Best Time
Anytime

---

*Why*
*Smiling can produce endorphins that can help your body with healing. When you visualize a smile in the light in the particular part of your body where you have a challenge, it activates powerful healing energy.*

# APPENDIX A

## Chant sounds

As mentioned in the first part of this book, some people like to use sounds with the techniques, while others do not. If you choose to use them, first chant the sound six times quietly enough that only you can hear it, then do it silently as many times as you'd like. Chanting can enhance the effectiveness of the technique, but it is not essential. At Spring Forest Qigong we believe that when you are doing qigong, or using these techniques, there is no right or wrong way; there is only good, better, or best.

These sounds don't translate easily from Chinese into English, so we've written them phonetically, with English spellings:

***Sheee*** (pronounced like "she," with the "e" sound lengthened)

> Hold your lips as though you're going to whistle and say "sheee."

> This sound connects to your liver system and is helpful for your liver, digestion, lymph system, eyes, and gallbladder.

***Kerrr*** (after an initial "k" sound, pronounced like the beginning of the word "earth" with the "rrr" lengthened)

> Purse your lips slightly when using this sound.

> "Kerrr" connects to your heart and is helpful for brain tumors and also for relationships in general. It assists with your small intestines and helps with digestion, gas, and acid reflux.

***Whooo*** (pronounced like the word "who," with the "oo" lengthened)

> This sound connects to your digestive system, stomach, spleen, and pancreas and is very helpful if you are involved in too much brain work.

**Seee** (pronounced like the word "see," with the "ee" lengthened)

Put the tip of your tongue behind the back of your upper teeth (not touching them) and say, "seee." The pronunciation of "Seee" differs slightly from the pronunciation of "Ceee" because of the placement of your tongue; you may not be able to hear the difference.

This sound works with your breathing system and is helpful for healing and cleansing your lymph system. It is useful for a runny nose, congestion, shoulder pain, chest pain, and gallbladder, lung, and eye problems.

"Seee" helps connect with more than 80 energy points in your lips, mouth, and tongue.

**Chueee** (pronounced "choo-ee" with the "choo" sound shorter and the accent on the lengthened "eee")

This sound focuses on your ears, kidneys, reproductive organs, and bladder and is helpful for bone density and bone marrow issues. It also assists in releasing fear and worry.

**Ceee** (pronounced like the word "see," with the "ee" lengthened)

Put the tip of your tongue at the bottom of your lower front teeth. Open your lips just a little, like a smile. Exhale gently, allowing your breath to flow softly over your lips. The pronunciation of "Ceee" differs slightly from the pronunciation of "Seee" because of the placement of your lips and tongue; you may not be able to hear the difference.

This sound helps with your pancreas and your lymph, digestive, and immune systems.

## APPENDIX B

### Lifestyles

If you sit at a computer a lot, if you are on your feet all day, or if you do physically strenuous labor, there are certain techniques that can help ease your daily stress and prevent or treat current health conditions.

**Sitting in front of a computer a lot: 2, 4, 5, 6, 21, 28, 31, 36, 55, 58, 63**

**Standing on your feet all day: 58, 60, 61**

**Working at physically demanding jobs: 28, 31, 56, 61**

# APPENDIX C

## Research

A new study by researchers from the University of Minnesota and one of the top Medical Centers in the United States has found that external qigong (as practiced by Chunyi Lin) helps patients' chronic pain.

The study states, "This is especially impressive given the long duration of pain in the majority of subjects." The peer-reviewed, randomized, controlled, clinical study was published in the August 2010 edition of the American Journal of Chinese Medicine.

Learn more at **www.springforestqigong.com/research.**

# INDEX

Heartburn, 19

Hips, 55, 58

Hormones, 52

Hot flashes, 52

**I**

Immune system, 1, 7, 14, 34, 42, 49

   In babies, 69, 70

Insomnia, 5, 7, 59 (*see also* Sleep)

   In babies, 69

**K**

Kidneys, 53, 56, 57

Knees, 55, 58

**L**

Legs, numbness of (legs "asleep"), 55, 64

Life force (see Kidneys, Energy)

Lifestyles, (see Lifestyles in Appendix B)

Liver, 33, 59, 75

Longevity, 18, 61

Lungs, 1, 3, 29, 30, 49, 50

   In babies, 66, 67

Lymph system, 14, 33, 34, 42, 49

   In babies, 69

**M**

Memory, 4, 17, 26, 47, 56

Menopause, 52, 56, 60, 61

Menstruation, 20, 41, 52, 56

Mental clarity (*see also* Brain), 4, 5, 7, 13, 22, 28

Motion sickness, 4, 8, 28

**N**

Nausea, 54

Neck, 3, 28, 48

Nervous system, 1, 15, 32

In babies, 68

Neuropathy, 32, 55

Nose (*see* Sinuses)

Nosebleeds, 29

**O**

Organs, opening blockages in, 22, 38

**P**

Pain

   Anywhere, 40

   Arm, 32

   Body, in general, 38

   Chest, 58

   Ear, 22

   Eye, 33

   Facial, 21, 24

   Head (*see* Headaches)

   Heart, 36

   Heart and chest, 34, 51

   Hip, 58

   Knees, 58

   Neck, 28, 48

   Rib, 58

   Sciatic nerve, 55, 58

   Shoulder, 48, 49

   Spinal, 31

   Stomach, 32, 72

Pancreas, 14, 50, 75

Panic attacks (*see* Anxiety)

Parkinson's Disease, 2

Pneumonia, 30, 50

Pregnancy, 73

Prostate, 18, 56, 57

**R**

Reproductive organs, 20, 35, 52, 56

**S**

Sciatic nerve, 55, 58

Scoliosis, 31

Seizures, 13

Sexual functioning, 53, 56

Shoulders, 3

Sinuses, 4, 11, 29, 30

Skin, 21, 33, 37

Sleep, (*see also* Insomnia), 5, 7, 26, 34, 54, 59

   Babies, 69

Smell, loss of sense of, 19

Spine, 31, 45, 48, 49

Spleen, 14

Stomach, 10, 14, 17, 32, 36, 54

   Babies, 67, 69

   Babies and small children, 72

Stress, 1, 3, 7, 15, 26, 28, 76

Stroke, 2, 26, 34, 41, 47, 56

Swelling, 40

## T

## U

## V

## W

## ABOUT SFQ

The vision of Spring Forest Qigong is "a healer in every family and a world without pain." Master Lin teaches that we are all born healers—not only healers of ourselves, but also healers of others. This can be as simple as bringing peaceful healing energy into your home or workplace by being a loving presence, or doing the energy-healing techniques that are taught in SFQ.

We teach four levels of Spring Forest Qigong. In the first level you learn seven simple active movements and a sitting meditation that help open the energetic channels in your body to enhance your energy and help you heal. At the end of Level One, we even teach you how to do the most basic healing techniques to help others heal. In Level Two through Level Four, you learn more advanced healing techniques to help others, along with deepening your understanding of Taoism and Traditional Chinese Medicine. You will also learn advanced meditations to enhance your own physical, mental, and spiritual health.

Along with teaching one of the most simple and effective qigong practices to be found, we also have a simple and unique holistic model of health. Most people talk about a mind/body/spirit model. We believe it is easier to understand, and a more accurate description, to call it a mind/body/heart model. In SFQ we concentrate on helping you quiet and focus your mind, relax your body, and direct your consciousness to your heart center. Here there is an energy, when activated, that not only helps open up your entire energetic body, but also leads to a full engagement with your life and then to a peace and joy that is available to all.

If you are interested in knowing more, we welcome you to discover how simple it can be to find health and healing, balance, and a more meaningful way of life with Spring Forest Qigong.

### See our website for lots of great information:
www.springforestqigong.com